PRAISE FOR *MAKE IT HAPPEN:*

"*Make It Happen* has made a positive impact in the way I approach training, competition, and life. Kyle blazed a new trail for Canadian gymnasts and showed us all that reaching the top of an Olympic podium is actually possible. He has been a difference maker in my life and his book continually filled me with new insights and fresh inspiration. I believe every athlete can benefit from reading it!"

*- **Ellie Black**, 2x Olympian, 2017 World AA Silver Medalist, 6x Commonwealth and 10x PanAm Medalist*

"*Make It Happen* is a must read for all athletes, parents and coaches. Kyle's journey is a great example of what it means to be athlete driven and parent/coach supported. I loved the honesty in which he shares his inner dialogue as he progressed and matured from a young tumbler to a world-class gymnast. This story is as much about Kyle's journey as a person as it is about his journey as an Olympic Champion."

*- **Marnie McBean**, OC OLY 3x Olympic Rowing Champion*

"Kyle Shewfelt is the only Canadian to become an Olympic champion in (what I consider) the world's most difficult athletic endeavour. In *Make It Happen*, he takes us on a very personal journey which led him to discover the enduring and undeniable power of sport."

*- **Scott Russell**, CBC Olympic Host*

"Kyle's account of a life in sport is honest and raw. It brought laughter, surprise, excitement, tears, and above all, hope. . . The glimpses of his parents' pragmatic and unwavering support, coupled with their commitment to raising a young man rather than an elite athlete, impacted me more than any how-to book on the same topic could ever accomplish. *Make It Happen* is compulsory reading for today's sport parent."

*- **Krista Thompson,** Parent*

"A refreshing account of self-discovery through sport. A true testament to how good coaching, honesty and resilience can lead to becoming one of the best in the world."

*- **Wayne McNeil,** Co-Founder of Respect Group*
(providers of Respect in Sport)

"Kyle Shewfelt's story is honest and engaging. I couldn't wait to turn the page to find out what happened next. This book is about so much more than gymnastics. It's about the strength of the human spirit, chasing big goals and believing in yourself to *make it happen*. Whether you're an athlete targeting the Olympics or someone aiming to complete their first 5KM on their path to becoming a runner, this book is full of valuable takeaways that can help everyone in their quest to cross their personal finish line."

*-**Kirsten-Ellen Fleming,** Executive Director, Run Calgary*

"Kyle is an inspiration to all. His raw candour about the challenges of the adolescent years, the complexity and sacrifice of high-performance sport, and the incredible reward of perseverance are all woven into this autobiography. It's clear that his coaches made a profound impact on his life and the stories of their positive approach are a valuable resource for the entire coaching community."

*- **Lorraine Lafrenière,** CEO, Coaching Association of Canada*

make it happen

\-

My Story of Gymnastics, the Olympics,
and the Positive Power of Sport

KYLE SHEWFELT

with Blythe Lawrence

The author has tried to recreate events, locales, and
conversations from his memories of them. In some
instances, conversations may not represent word-
for-word transcripts. The author has tried to retell
them in a way that evokes the feeling and meaning
of what was said and, in all instances, he believes
the essence of the dialogue to be accurate.

For information on special discounts for bulk purchases
and fundraising, please contact info@kyleshewfelt.com.

Front cover image: Adrian Dennis/AFP/Getty Images
Back cover image: The Canadian Press/Adrian Wyld
All interior photos are courtesy of the Shewfelt family
unless otherwise noted
Author image: Phil Crozier

Printed and bound in Canada by Friesens

MIX
Paper from
responsible sources
FSC® C016245
www.fsc.org

ISBN
978-0-2288-2441-1 (Hardcover)
978-0-2288-2440-4 (Paperback)
978-0-2288-2442-8 (eBook)

To Nora

Through it all, I'll be right there to support you.
I love you more than I love gymnastics.

CONTENTS

PREFACE

THIS BOOK WAS A WORK IN PROGRESS FOR THE better part of a decade. I began the writing process in 2010, but lost my momentum because I didn't have a clear reason why I was writing it. Sure, I had a fun collection of reflections and memories, but a central theme was missing. Then, in January 2019, things became clearer: sport has had a positive impact on my life and illuminating the experiences and people that helped shape that perspective is important. And with this overarching purpose secure in my mind, the book came together like a great floor routine. I truly hope that my story can ignite a conversation about the positive power of sport.

When I was a kid, I craved behind-the-scenes stories from my Olympic idols. I'd wonder: *What did they do the day they won the Olympics? How did they deal with the pressure and expectations? How did they stay motivated? Did they ever act out or want to quit? What happened at all those after-parties?* I'm sharing my journey in hopes that others can learn from it and that I can give something back. If one person reads this book and is brought a step closer to achieving their goal(s), then my mission has been accomplished.

As a father, the only wish I have for my daughter is that she finds the thing that makes her heart smile, whatever that may be. When I finally found gymnastics and declared that I wanted to be an Olympic champion, my parents never questioned that dream. They supported it and I look back on their dedication with deep appreciation. I plan on revisiting these pages throughout my own parenting journey to be reminded of the incredible example my parents set for me. They were always encouraging, yet they also allowed me to experience failure. I hope I've captured the importance of their unwavering commitment. If one parent reads this book and discovers a new strategy to help their child, then my mission has been accomplished.

I was surrounded by many special coaches during my career, including my long-time personal coach, Kelly Manjak. He and I still talk frequently, and he is one of the first people I call when I have news to share or a problem to solve. To me, Kelly is everything a coach should aim to be: a friend, a mentor, a motivator, an advocate, and a source of accountability. I hope his magic shines through and that the coaching philosophies featured here encourage others to take a similar athlete-centred approach. If one coach reads this book and can see a new path, then my mission has been accomplished.

Building this project has been an adventure and paying tribute to many of the difference makers in my life has been so rewarding. Thank you to everyone for your endless support!

Kyle Shewfelt
Calgary, 2020

PROLOGUE: THE LANDING

Stuttgart, Germany
World Gymnastics Championships
August 27, 2007

BY 9 A.M. THE TRAINING GYM WAS ALIVE WITH quiet activity. Gymnasts from different countries were warming up: swinging on the high bar, circling around the pommel horse, and flying down the vault runway. Lined up around the apparatus and awaiting their turn, some joked quietly with their teammates, but for the most part everyone was serious and focused on their routines. The *pat-pat-pat* of running footsteps, the crack of the springboard, the thud of feet landing on stiff mats, and the hiss of hand grips on the high bar as guys swung into their dismounts were the only sounds to be heard.

Hovering off to the side of landing mats, tight-lipped coaches in national team tracksuits observed each gymnast closely as he moved through his routine. Every now and then, one would quietly confer with an athlete, then the gymnast would nod and get back in line. The gym, part of a big athletic dome, had high concrete ceilings and fluorescent lights. Almost imperceptibly, small flakes of chalk dust rose into the air, floating softly toward the ceiling.

We were training at 9 a.m. because we would be competing at 9 a.m. It was always like that at big competitions. The theory is that the body gets used to doing a certain thing at a certain time every day, which is important when you're launching yourself ten feet into the air several times in the space of seventy seconds.

Edouard Iarov, the Canadian national coach, gave us two days to get acclimated to the seven-hour time difference between our pre-Worlds training-camp base in Calgary and Germany. On the third, he called for full routines. That morning each of us warmed up and signalled to Edouard when we were ready to show a full set. His penetrating gaze added an extra layer of pressure. If you could do it with Edouard watching, you knew you could do it in competition when it really mattered.

When I felt fully warmed up, I showed Edouard my floor routine. It was a good one, among the best I'd done since the Athens Olympics three years earlier. As I landed my dismount, a smattering of applause echoed off the concrete walls and I felt a little rush of pride. In training, everyone watches others with half a mind, focusing on what they need to do. Those spontaneous bursts of applause only happen when someone does something really impressive.

I knew the routine had been good. I'd gotten into a nice groove leading up to the World Championships. Everything was falling into place, I reflected happily over breakfast that morning. After the post-Olympic roller coaster, I struggled to manage the new expectations placed on my shoulders, but I was finally back where I was most comfortable: chasing a dream. *I may be the Olympic champion, but I'm not the reigning world champion,* I told myself. *Here's my chance.*

But to achieve that goal, the routine I'd just done might not be enough. If I performed a harder variation of my opening Arabian double front tumbling pass, I knew I'd bank more difficulty points with the judges. Keeping my body straight in the air as opposed to piking it changed the whole dynamic of the skill, making it about five times harder. More of the body's surface area would be exposed to air drag, slowing down rotation. Additionally, my head would be arched back, so I'd be landing "blind," meaning I wouldn't see the floor before my feet touched ground. It was officially called a Tamayo, first performed by Charles Tamayo of Cuba, and only a handful of gymnasts had ever attempted this skill.

The reward for all this risk would be an additional 0.1 added to my difficulty score, but I knew from experience that this small margin could make the difference between winning a world title and walking away empty-handed. "Edouard," I called. "I'm going to do a couple of Arabian double layouts." He nodded. Though it had been good, the routine I'd just shown was playing it safe, and we both knew it. It was time to go for broke.

I stepped into the corner of the floor and raised my arms. *Ready.* I took four quick steps and hurdled into my roundoff, snapping my arms up over my head. *Set.* The gym whirled around as I flipped into the back handspring. Floor, ceiling, and floor again whizzed by in a blur and I punched hard off the mat, launching into the big skill. *Go!*

That's when I made the mistake.

As I lifted off the ground and turned my body over, I was just a little bit lower than I'd intended—an inch, two at the most—but I didn't know it as I took off, and wouldn't realize it for another second, the time it took for me to collide with the mat, heels first.

I expected to float back down to earth in complete control, landing like I was sitting in an invisible chair. The actual landing came as a terrible jolt. My legs jammed into the floor with the force of a car crash. The awful thud of bone impacting bone and the sickening crack of my knees hyperextending reverberated straight up my spine and into my brain. My head snapped forward and my chin thudded hard into my chest as I crumpled to the floor in a heap. Somewhere very far away I heard people gasp.

For a split second, I couldn't feel anything below my hips. *I've fallen into a hole,* I thought, dazed. *Why is there a hole in the floor?*

Then, like cylinders firing through an engine, pain exploded through the lower half of my body.

A still, terrifying silence settled over the training gym as everyone stopped and turned to look at me lying on the ground. Vaguely, it occurred to me that there would be no applause for what I'd just done.

The pain was excruciating. Instinctively, my body curled into the fetal position. I was able to bend my legs to my chest, but they locked up and wouldn't move after that. I whimpered and moaned, feeling my eyes rolling around in my head. Concerned faces moved in and out of my line of vision, blocking the glare of the fluorescent lights high above. Edouard. Then my personal coach, Tony Smith, and the team's red-haired physical therapist, Susan Massitti. Then our massage therapist, Ed Louie. Finally, a German doctor and a small battalion of volunteers, all wearing matching baby-blue polo shirts. In my peripheral vision my teammates looked on, anxiety written all over their faces.

It took Susan, Ed, and the doctor five minutes to straighten my legs, and every millimetre of movement was torture. My legs felt like they were made of metal. With each small amount of progress, expletives fell from my lips as I stifled screams. Inside my head, thoughts appeared and disappeared as though as they were being fed through one of those red View-Master toys from my childhood.

I'm never going to walk again. Click.

No, I'll be fine, I probably just need some ice. Click.

This is the Olympic team qualifier. The Olympics are eleven months away. Click.

I have to compete. Click.

If Canada doesn't qualify to the Games it will be all my fault. Click.

I'm walking out of here. Click.

Holy sh--, this hurts!

After several minutes they managed to hoist me into a sitting position. Two people stepped up and put my arms around their shoulders, then carried me to a bench beside the floor. My legs dangled uselessly beneath me. They felt very hot.

Very gently, the doctor pressed a wand-like instrument against my knees. "This is a mini-ultrasound machine," he explained. "It will indicate damage to the ACL and MCL, the important ligaments in the knees." He and Susan conferred in low tones as he read the results.

"They're going to call a car to take you to the hospital for more tests," Susan announced. "Someone's going to bring a wheelchair. They'll wheel you out."

"No," I said. I couldn't bear to leave the training gym in a wheelchair. Foolish or not, I wasn't going to be defeated by what had happened.

"I don't want a wheelchair," I told her. "I'm walking out of here." Suddenly, that seemed so important. If I could just walk out of the gym, whatever I'd done couldn't be that bad. Susan shook her head, but as a Canadian Olympic speedskater herself, she understood that I was desperately trying to gain the upper hand.

My legs felt twangy as they touched the ground. Out of nowhere, crutches appeared under my armpits. Susan and the doctor supported me as I inched my way out of the gym. Just before reaching the door, I glanced back. The last thing I saw was my teammates strapping on their wrist guards and preparing to move to the next event. They still had a job to do. Canada's Olympic qualification hung in the balance.

• • •

By the time they slid me into the tube-like MRI (magnetic resonance imaging) machine, my legs were swelling. *At this rate, they're going to get so big I'll be stuck in here.* I lay there for the next twenty minutes, oscillating between optimism and disbelief.

My mind ran through all potential scenarios. *This is just a minor blip on the radar. I'll be good in a couple of days and still be able to compete. What if this was the last day I ever tumble? What about my team? What about Beijing?* I tried to visualize my routines, but the pain pulsating through my legs was just too distracting.

They propped me up on a table beside the MRI machine while an orthopaedic doctor looked at the scans. When another wheelchair appeared I made a move to get up, but someone's arm held me back. "I don't want that," I objected. "I want to walk."

"You shouldn't have walked in here," the doctor replied. "And I'm sorry, but you're not walking out. You've broken both of your legs. You will definitely not be competing here in Germany."

Both of my legs? The impact of the landing had made the two bones around my kneecaps hyperextend and crash into each other, he explained. In each knee, the top bone had hit the bottom one, fracturing the tibia. The force of the diagnosis hit me as hard as the landing, and suddenly I couldn't hold back the tears. Susan rubbed my back sympathetically as tears began streaming down my cheeks and my shoulders heaved with sobs.

After the 2004 Olympics, I'd struggled to find the motivation to continue gymnastics. You're on top of the world when you win gold and after that there's nowhere to go but down. Before Athens, I'd been the chaser, my dream of becoming an Olympic champion pulling me through every minute of every day. But after, I'd just felt afraid: afraid of making mistakes, afraid of letting everyone down.

It took breaking both of my legs to free me of that. The moment I received the diagnosis, I realized just how much I wanted to go back to the Olympics. *This can't be the way my story ends*, I thought. I am going to go out and get it—again.

Just as soon as I can stand up and walk.

1

CARTWHEELS

IN CANADIAN HOSPITAL DELIVERY ROOMS FROM Victoria to Yellowknife to Charlottetown, many a father gazes into his newborn son's eyes and pictures him growing up to be the next Wayne Gretzky or Sidney Crosby. Wes Shewfelt was no different, but having been a semi-professional hockey player himself, perhaps he had a better reason to imagine than most.

My father was born in Basswood, Manitoba, a hamlet of 100 people on the Canadian prairie between Saskatoon and Winnipeg. His mother owned the town's general store, and he grew up right above it. His early life revolved around hockey. Every day after school, my dad and his buddies headed down to the local outdoor rink to play pick-up hockey and blast pucks around. The way my father tells it, you knew it was time to head home for dinner when you could no longer feel your toes.

On the weekends, Basswood boys piled into a car to go play league games in nearby Rapid City. By the time he was fifteen, my dad was playing on four different teams, spanning age-group to collegiate levels, all at the same time. In the box between periods, he did his ninth-grade homework.

The letter from the Brandon Wheat Kings, a team in the Western Hockey League, inviting him to a selection camp arrived shortly after he began winning MVP awards, and Dad made the cut on his second try. In his one season playing for Brandon, he came to two conclusions.

Number one: as much as he loved the game, he didn't have the skill to play in the NHL.

Number two: small-town Manitoba could not give him the life he wanted.

A year later, at age eighteen, he and some friends packed up a car and made the twelve-hour drive to Calgary, where he eventually landed a job at the Canadian Imperial Bank of Commerce.

He didn't completely give up on hockey. He joined the local beer league, where post-game beer chugging was taken as seriously as what happened on the ice. One of the men in the league was a big, gregarious guy named Hugh "Tack" Tackaberry, and at a party on New Year's Eve of 1973, someone introduced Dad to Tack's little sister.

Nola Tackaberry was a formidable young woman who had graduated from high school at sixteen, having done three grades in two years when she was younger. She also loved to bowl and was a part of a local league, though rolling a three-pound ball toward five pins was the extent of her athletic abilities. A few days into 1974, my father's phone rang. Nola was looking for a lift to a hockey game—could he take her? That car ride was their beginning; eight months later they were engaged. They married in Calgary on July 10, 1976. Two children followed: my older brother Scott was born on March 26, 1980, and I came along two years later, on May 6, 1982.

We lived on a cul-de-sac near a park in a community called Dover in the southeastern quarter of Calgary. Dover has a reputation as one of the rougher parts of the city, a place where many families struggle to make ends meet. Some people refer to it as the "hood" because of its higher crime rate and lower socioeconomic status, but my parents bought a house in Dover the year after they were married and they still live there today.

Scott and I were active, rambunctious children. One of my earliest memories involves us putting our underwear on our heads and running around the house pretending to be Spider-Man. My brother liked to chase me around on all fours, pretending to be Kimba the White Lion from the popular Japanese anime series on TV. Our favourite game was to pile all of the couch cushions and blankets in the house at the bottom of the basement stairs and launch ourselves onto them from the top step. When the weather was good, we romped around exploring with the neighbourhood kids. In the winter, we went tobogganing; summers were spent on family camping trips and vacations at Minnedosa Lake.

Naturally, we were a hockey family. As soon as we could walk, Dad took us to the local rink and attached strap-on skates to our feet. He would hold us up as he skated around, giving us a feel for the ice. I could skate before I was two and recall, even as a very young child, how much I enjoyed whooshing around the rink, the wind cold on my cheeks.

Unfortunately, that was the only thing I liked about it.

Canadian boys begin their hockey careers early. Not long after my fifth birthday, I was put onto the ice at the East Calgary Twin Arena with a group of kids from my neighbourhood for a team tryout. The coaches put us through basic drills to see how we stacked up against each other, then ranked us accordingly. I spent the whole time flying around the rink, keen to show everyone how I could skate backwards. All the boys made a team in the end, but I must have impressed someone, because I was put on Scott's team, skipping the beginner league entirely.

Looking back, the league may have just made an exception so my parents would only have to drive to one practice, but I remember feeling very pleased at being fast-tracked onto the big boys' team. Even at five, being pinpointed and recognized made me feel special. But as the months wore on, I came to realize there was something missing in my new activity. Pulsating adrenalin, an all-consuming desire to be the best, those nerves that make you want to simultaneously dance around an arena and throw up in the nearest trash can—all that was missing with hockey. It wasn't until years later that I could look back and identify the problem as a lack of passion.

Any flicker of interest I'd had in the sport was quickly snuffed out. Waking up at 5:30 a.m. to go to practice on Saturdays got old fast. When someone passed me the puck, I had no idea what to do with it. During face-offs, I spent more time waving at my family in the stands—where I could usually pick out my Grandma Trude, my number one fan—than anticipating the puck drop. I couldn't score a goal to save my life. Dad had to bribe me with Slurpees, Denver omelette sandwiches, and five-cent candies from the arena's concession stand to get me to go to practice. For the better part of three years, I played a large role in keeping the concession stand in business. And without realizing it, I began looking around for an activity I could really get excited about.

. . .

In our backyard that summer, Scott taught me to do a cartwheel. It was a revelation, akin to learning to walk, and I loved it immediately. Cartwheeling became my new way of getting from point A to point B. It got to the point where I spent almost as much time on my hands as on my feet. My most vivid childhood memories all involve cartwheeling: in the kitchen, across the living room, down the hallway, or outside on the front lawn. Careening upside down through space was like gliding over the ice, but a thousand times better.

Cartwheels were just the beginning. Soon after I also discovered new uses for furniture. Beds were suddenly more than just places to sleep; the bedsprings could catapult me almost to the ceiling and provide a soft landing pad for front flips. Walls turned into supports for handstands. I became addicted to the freedom of flying through the air.

A few months later, I taught myself my first serious gymnastics move. Standing on the grass in the backyard, I swung my arms and bent my knees, then launched myself backwards onto my hands. I had no idea that there was a name—a back handspring—for what I was doing. All I knew was that it was thrilling!

Once I had learned to do one flip, I wanted to do two in a row. That wasn't as easy, but because I was willing to try it a thousand times, I eventually figured it out and savoured the accomplishment of mastering something new. I had found an activity that filled me with joy, though I still didn't know what it was. I just knew it was loads more fun than hockey.

Mom felt a little differently. My cartwheels tended to be noisy—I had the habit of screaming "Weeeeeeeeeeeee!" with glee as I went around. Several times, she narrowly avoided getting a foot in the face while taking dinner out of the oven or crossing the kitchen to get to the basement staircase. Once, in the throes of a tumbling routine, my cartwheeling nearly knocked her over as she was carrying hot dishes to the table. Worse, I just avoided landing inside the open red-hot oven.

That was enough for Mom, who decided that if I was going to flip around, I was going to do it in a safe environment. After dinner one evening, she sat down with the local phone book, licked her finger, and flicked through the pages until she found the heading for gymnastics clubs. The first club on the list was the Altadore Gymnastic Club. She dialed the number.

"I have a hyperactive six-year-old boy," she announced to the person who answered the phone. "Please help save my furniture." Five minutes later, I was enrolled in the beginner class.

Something clicked the very first day I walked into Altadore. As I looked wide-eyed from one end of the gym to the other, I saw possibility. The gym was a wonderland of plush mats of all colours and shapes and sizes, with a huge blue floor carpet and all kinds of neat contraptions to climb on and jump off. I was thrilled to discover the big blue floor had springs under it that made it bouncy, a lot like a trampoline.

It was the giant playground I had been longing for as I flipped around the kitchen, nearly setting myself on fire. Nothing in the world could have pleased me more.

• • •

At the time, Altadore was divided into two gyms. One side housed the competitive program. The other side was for the recreational gymnasts, kids who were beginners or in it for fitness and fun. A wall separated the two.

I started out in the recreational program. From the big viewing room where parents sat during classes you could watch the competitive kids train, but when you were down on the floor of the rec gym you could only see the other side through a small archway in the wall. That archway came to represent the portal to another world, one I desperately wanted to be a part of. Sometimes I would stand just inside the arch and watch wistfully as the gymnasts in the competitive program worked out. It felt like a separate universe, near but so far away.

Gyms are rarely glamorous today, and in the 1980s they were even less so. Altadore, in a warehouse in the industrial part of town, had a big Rocky Balboa vibe. The competitive side of the gym smelled like dirty feet and musty old foam blocks, but to me it was magical. The flipping and flying and energetic buzz lit the place up from one wall to the other. I enjoyed the rec classes immensely, but also felt very curious about the competitive side. *I'll be over there one day*, I promised myself.

In the meantime, the rec program helped me build physical literacy and foster a strong foundation. After a few sessions, I was moved into the "superman" group reserved for the bigger and more advanced boys. I was anything but big; indeed, I was small for my age, skinny and slight. The most noticeable thing was that I wore my light blond hair perfectly parted and slicked to the side with gel, an early manifestation of the perfectionist streak that would both serve and torment me in the years that followed.

The other boys in my new group were a few years older than I was, and I was desperate to impress them. On my first day in their group, as soon as the coaches told us we could go out on the floor, I barreled out at full speed and flew across the mat, careening around hula hoops and pylons before launching into my biggest trick: a roundoff back handspring.

The ploy got the other boys' attention. "Whoa! That was awesome, little buddy. You're so good!" one of the bigger guys yelled. I grinned shyly, my heart swelling with happiness.

The rec program had a few different coaches, but it was a young guy named Brian who brought Kelly Manjak into my life. Brian took an appraising look at me and after a few classes asked Kelly, the competitive boys head coach, to come see what I could do.

"There's a little boy in my rec group and you need to take him," Brian told Kelly. "He belongs in your competitive program. He's a super talent."

As we were tumbling on the floor one day a few weeks later, a tall man came through the archway and walked straight toward me. Kelly was the image of 1980s masculinity. He wore a navy athletic jacket, shorts, and white knee-high socks. The jacket had a red stripe down the arms, with "Altadore Gymnastic Club" printed on the back in bold red letters. Best of all, he had a rad mullet. Totally cool, I thought (hey, I was six and it was the '80s). He crouched down beside me and stuck out a giant hand.

"Hi Kyle," he said, flashing a friendly crooked grin. "My name is Kelly."

I immediately liked his voice. There was a comforting gentleness in it. "Hi," I said shyly, timidly shaking his big paw of a hand.

"Say, your coach Brian told me that you can do a back handspring," Kelly said enthusiastically. "Is that true? Can you show me?"

I nodded. "Sure," I said eagerly. I leapt to my feet and moved to the edge of the floor for my full-speed run up. I imagined my feet whirling like Fred Flintstone's when he drove his prehistoric foot-powered car in the cartoon and hurdled into my best roundoff back handspring. I landed on my feet and looked up to see Kelly's smiling face, his blue eyes slightly wider than before.

"Wow!" he said, genuine admiration in his voice. "That was pretty darn good. Where did you learn to do that?"

"In my backyard," I answered with a grin, glowing from the praise.

"Holy cow. That's a pretty good back handspring for learning it in your backyard, Kyle. Good job. How about your splits, how are those?"

Pleased as punch that this guy was taking so much interest in my skills, I jumped right down into the splits, making sure to show Kelly my best side, left leg forward.

"Geez, those are some nice splits, little man!" he said enthusiastically. "How about pull-ups? Let's go over to the bar and see how many you can do." He lumbered across the gym and I followed eagerly behind like a little blond Labrador puppy trailing a Great Dane.

When Kelly lifted me to the bar, I made two pull-ups and bicycled my legs trying to do a third. "You've got to do them with your toes pointed and your feet glued together," Kelly counselled. "That's how gymnasts do pull-ups." He picked a small block of foam off the ground and placed it between my feet. "Squeeze this with your feet and give it another try."

I squeezed and began again. Kelly's tip did indeed make it easier, and in the end I did seven. Kelly was beaming as I jumped down. "You're flexible, acrobatic, *and* strong, too!" he exclaimed.

As I nodded with a smirky little smile, Kelly uttered the three little words all coaches say when they spot a potentially talented athlete.

"Where's your mom?" he asked pleasantly.

"She's out there," I said, pointing to the viewing area.

"I'd like to talk to her," he said.

As we walked off the floor and into the waiting area, Kelly put his hand on my shoulder, like a father to a son. During those few steps, a trust sprang up between us. He had found his athlete. I had found my coach. This was exactly how it was meant to be. Our Olympic journey had officially begun.

2

GOLDEN FISH

IN HIS STUDENT DAYS IN CRANBROOK, BRITISH Columbia, Kelly Manjak wanted to be a gymnast. The problem was that at 6'1", he was so tall that when he swung on the high bar he had to bend his legs just so his feet didn't scrape the floor. That alone ruled out any real future as a national level competitor, but it didn't deter Kelly. If he couldn't be a high-level gymnast, he figured maybe he could coach them. So he applied himself to that.

By the time we met in 1988, Kelly was in charge of the competitive men's program at Altadore. He privately referred to his up-and-coming group of boys as the Chinese Men's Group. The Chinese were one of the best teams in the world, and Kelly wanted us to grow up to be just like them. At six, I was one of the youngest in the group. After meeting Kelly, I started going to gymnastics twice a week for two hours at a time. A few months later, when I turned seven, I moved to three two-hour long sessions per week, and by eight I was training three hours a day, four times a week. Twelve hours was a fair amount for an eight-year-old, but it still left plenty of time for getting into trouble outside the gym.

Mom believed that if we were confined to flipping around outside, her dinners would be safe and I would be less likely to wind up in the oven. To that end, Scott and I got a backyard trampoline—an octagon with blue and yellow pads—for Christmas in 1990. I couldn't get enough of it.

I also started to catch gymnastics on TV a few times a year, which gave me my first look at what the world's best were capable of. Canadian champion Curtis Hibbert, the Americans, and the Soviets quickly became my role models. I also admired the rock stars of women's gymnastics: Canadian Stella Umeh, Americans Kim Zmeskal and Shannon Miller, and the great Svetlana Boguinskaia, referred to as the "Belarusian swan." Inspired by what I saw, I would run outside to get in two or three routines on the trampoline during commercial breaks, pretending I was in the meet too.

Watching high-level gymnastics brought out the little daredevil in me. Though Altadore was equipped with spotting belts and a pit filled with foam blocks and my backyard was not, I made no distinction between the two. One day, after seeing the Canadian Gymnastics Championships on television, I randomly decided I was ready for double backflips, where a gymnast turns his body over twice in the air before landing on his feet.

Just in case it all went wrong, I stacked a bunch of knitted afghan blankets and old pillows in the middle of the trampoline. Standing at one end, I bounced higher and higher, and after one big punch, shot my arms up and threw my legs over my head, soaring up and backwards. I almost made it. I got one and three quarters of the way around before landing on my face, followed in very short order by my hands and knees. The impact sent my face skidding across the trampoline, stopping right next to my makeshift landing zone.

"My God, Kyle, what happened to your face?" Kelly asked the next day. Trampoline burn—essentially a rug burn—ran in one angry red line from my forehead to my chin.

"I was trying to do double backs on my trampoline, and I kind of landed on my forehead and slid," I explained, embarrassed.

"That's not safe—" Kelly began.

"But I was *being* safe," I insisted. "I put blankets and pillows in the middle of the trampoline. I just missed them by an inch, but I was super close to landing it." Kelly opened his mouth like he wanted to say more, but all that came out was a laugh.

• • •

The trampoline wasn't the only thing endangering my head. At hockey, the black projectile whizzed by, inches from my nose, before banging to a stop at the back of the net. With a sigh, I got to my feet. I was wearing a mask, but that did not make playing goalie feel any safer.

There was a rule on my team that everyone got to play goalie for a game, which really meant that everyone *had* to play goalie for a game. My heart jumped in terror every time the coach announced who it would be, and I prayed they would just forget about me.

They didn't, but it was literally their loss. In my first and only appearance in the net, I let in thirteen goals, giving the other team a lopsided victory even by beginner league standards.

Gymnastics was going great, but hockey became more and more of a struggle. I didn't give a flying puck about whether or not we won a game. All I could think during hockey practice was how I would rather be playing at the gym.

Mom initiated the conversation one night at the kitchen table as I pushed peas around on my plate. "Kelly called today and asked if you wanted to move up to sixteen hours a week," she said, heaping my plate with a spoonful of vegetables.

I brightened up immediately. "Yes!" I squealed.

"But Kyle, if you do that, I don't think you'll be able to continue to do both gymnastics and hockey," she continued. "You're starting to miss a lot of hockey practice anyway because of all the gymnastics." When I didn't say anything, she continued, "Of course, it's up to you. What do you want to do?"

Easygoing as always, my parents had left the choice up to me. Gymnastics or hockey was my first real decision in life, and it was a no-brainer.

"Gymnastics, of course," I said quickly. "I don't mind giving up hockey. Really." I jumped up from the table and cartwheeled off excitedly before Mom could call me back to finish the meal. No more hockey! With that, the skates dropped off my feet and out of my life, leaving me free to run, jump, and flip to my heart's content.

• • •

Quitting hockey meant that Saturday mornings at the rink were exchanged for Saturday mornings in warehouses all over Alberta. I began competing at a beginner level in 1990, about two years after joining Kelly's team.

I was a born competitor. There was something about the meet that made me better. When it was do or die, I did, and at the end of the day I often found myself standing atop a victory podium. During the time it took to do my routines, things were glorious, but I soon became afraid of making mistakes and subsequently losing. The thought of failing was bothersome at first. Later on, it would haunt me.

We competed against several other gyms in the area. The best was the University of Calgary Gymnastics Club, whose boys were coached by a man named Tony Smith. The U of C boys were always the most physically prepared for competitions and showed off an impressive array of difficult skills. Though technically rivals, Kelly and Tony were friends with the common goal of developing a strong Alberta provincial team. That didn't mean Tony and I immediately hit it off.

Led by Kelly, Tony, and a few others, the best boys in the province gathered for a special training camp a few times a year. Part of each camp was dedicated to testing us on strength, flexibility, and skill level. One test was to climb a rope to the ceiling as fast as possible, but because rope climbs weren't part of Kelly's normal conditioning routine, I wasn't familiar with them. The climb up was no problem, but I must have lost my grip near the top because the next thing I knew I was hurtling through the air toward the hard mats twenty feet below. Thankfully I wasn't physically injured, though the memory did leave a scar. To this day, this fall still pops into my head every time I'm at the top of the rope.

Tony was sitting right there, and although he could see the fall had shaken me up, his mouth tightened with displeasure. I saw him looking disappointed and felt tears well up in my eyes.

"I don't want to do it again," I whimpered. That didn't please Tony, who at that point in his career was a "boys don't cry" type of coach. Kelly, meanwhile, briskly strode over, scooped me up, and checked to make sure I was okay. He didn't let me out of his sight for the rest of the day.

"I think we'll get a rope at our gym so we can practice before the next testing day and build you some confidence," he mused. "How does that sound?" I nodded and sniffled, grateful for his understanding. He was going to protect me.

. . .

"3 . . . 2 . . . 1 . . . blast-off!" Scott yelled. In four steps, he had run over the peak of the roof and launched himself off into space.

Our outdoor stunts got more daring as we got bigger. We figured out that we could climb the backyard fence and edge along toward the garage, then jump up onto the roof. From there, we could skip over the low-hanging power lines and onto the trampoline below, a drop of about six feet.

Scott always did a bum drop, landing in a sitting position on the trampoline with his legs straight out in front of him. When he moved off to the side, I ran and leapt off the roof, swan diving head first. At the last moment, I turned my body over and landed on the trampoline on my back, pinging myself straight upwards. That never got old.

I think this game made my mom a little nervous, so when Kelly and I proposed upping our hours in the gym to twenty per week, she agreed readily.

Not all of this time in the gym was spent tumbling, swinging, and sweating. To Kelly, being able to do a skill was only half the battle—you also had to make it look nice. "Artistic gymnastics means it has to be polished as well as powerful," he told us. He coached us on the way our posture should look when we stood in a corner of the floor and made us practice saluting the judges in a mirror. Kelly wanted to see our feet together, tight legs, chest tall, tailbone tucked, chin up, eyes looking to the end of the floor, perfectly parallel lines, sharp arms with all fingers stretched out and thumbs tucked in. And all that was before we began our routines.

To improve our form, Kelly insisted that the Chinese Men's Group take ballet once a week. Some guys might have found it was a waste of time to do ballet, but I accepted it as an important part of training. Ballet classes involved a lot of flexibility work, lifting our legs to our noses and holding them in place, as well as special attention to toe point, leg extension, and posture. As we stood at the barre, our teacher, a lovely redheaded lady named Lydia, walked down the line straightening our hips and lifting our legs just a little bit higher.

"If you don't wear gymnastics shorts to class so I can see your knees, you're all going to do ballet in your underwear!" Lydia would announce cheerfully at some point during every class. When one of the boys obstinately wore sweatpants to the next one, Lydia followed through on her threat. We seven boys did ballet in our undies and T-shirts that day.

Ballet was a lot more fun than death conditioning, the other weekly staple of our training program. Death conditioning was a strength training program imposed on us by Kelly's mentor Eugene Galperin, a small Russian man who had come to Canada from the Soviet Union. Eugene had been a very successful coach in the USSR and was one of the first to introduce the Soviet system of gymnastics to Canada. Kelly met him at a clinic in Toronto in the early 1990s.

"What do you want?" Eugene asked him bluntly the first time they met. "I want to create world-class athletes," Kelly responded equally bluntly. Eugene must have admired such unbridled ambition, because after that he agreed to come to Altadore for two weeks every summer to give us a taste of Soviet-style training. Kelly never assumed he knew it all—he was a very young coach, still in his early twenties, and he had a lot to learn.

Dressed in his red Adidas tracksuit, Eugene cut an intimidating figure. There was no cheating and no excuses with him. We always tried a little harder to do well when Eugene was around. We stood a little straighter and dug deeper to finish those challenging assignments. Eugene was trying to create great gymnasts and it was his job to teach Kelly how to do this in an intense but healthy way. Encouraging us to go beyond our comfort zones was the only way we'd reach our ultimate potential.

We called it death conditioning because you wanted to die, or at least puke, afterwards. Eugene's program was a combination of exercises designed to build our endurance and power while also working basic elements. It included repeating a variety of tasks in succession, an endless series of sprints, handstand push-ups, rope climbs, muscle-ups, dips, back handsprings, pommel horse circles, and swings to handstand on parallel bars. The goal was to complete the list as quickly as possible, finishing with a full lap of the gym, stairs included, in the wheelbarrow position on your hands with a teammate or coach supporting your legs.

The point of this challenging regimen was to push our bodies and minds to their limit, to find out how much capacity we had. The experiment was always conducted during the final hour of the last practice of the week, when a day of rest and recovery was on the horizon. It was hard physical work, but nobody ever forced us to do it, nor were we ever pushed to finish it if it got too hard. It was extreme, but Eugene believed that enduring the pain and suffering brought on by such intense physical work would make you stronger mentally and physically. After just a few weeks, we *did* feel stronger and were able to do more. Get through that, and your stamina and mental fortitude at the end of a competition was rarely in question, or so Eugene's theory went.

Those weeks with Eugene would set us up for the rest of the year. He had plans and books and a million drills in his back pocket. He believed that measuring was motivating, so he tacked charts on the wall that described the different levels and what skills boys should have mastered by different ages on each event. Each boy on the team had his name on one axis and all of the skills listed on the other. The first time you attempted one of the new skills, you got to colour in half the box. Only when you showed real mastery and could do it nine times out of ten with impeccable form and confidence could you colour in the other half in this game of gymnastics bingo. The goal was to get a blackout, or mastering every skill that fell within your age range.

The charts stayed up when Eugene left, and whenever I looked at them I felt as if Eugene was somehow peering out at me. I always felt proud when I mastered a skill beyond my years and got to colour in the box all the way, which typically happened on floor and vault, my two best events.

The first time Eugene came to Altadore, I was nine years old. During his first practice, Eugene pointed to me and in his thick Russian accent said, "Is that blond boy the one you telling me about?"

"That's him," Kelly affirmed.

"This boy is golden fish," Eugene declared. "He's not like others. He is super talent. But you need to protect this one. He needs kindness and care, and long-term plan."

For good measure, he looked at Kelly and added: "And if he becomes nothing, you are horrible coach."

3

PERFECT 10

IN 1991, THE HOURS AND NUMBERS WE'D BEEN doing in the gym began to pay off. I found my groove when competing, so much so that something extraordinary happened: on one of my compulsory floor routines that year, I earned a perfect 10.

Tens were rare, especially for compulsory exercises—routines where every gymnast does the same skills in the same order. Compulsories are boring for everyone. Judges and parents watch the same thing over and over and try not to fall asleep. The gymnasts, many of whom are in the sport because they have an abundance of energy, get restless waiting hours between turns. But there I was, canning a perfect score. I was only nine, but after the news of the perfect 10 got around, people began watching me a little more closely.

Getting a ten meant you had done something outstanding. I was shy and shrugged it off, but inside I knew that I had earned the score. I had been meticulous in going over all the details. I had done ten routines a day, aiming for perfection with each one. Usually at the end of a routine you instantly think of at least one thing that could have been better, but this was one of the rare occasions when I knew I couldn't have done anything more. The achievement left me feeling a unique and unfamiliar high.

A few months later, Kelly, Mom, and I piled into her white Ford Tempo and drove eight hours through a blizzard to my first out-of-province competition, the Taiso Invitational in Saskatoon, Saskatchewan. I was so nervous I couldn't eat breakfast before the meet, but I did well, sweeping the seven gold medals available. That got people talking a little more. Soon after, Altadore was contacted by the local news affiliate, 2&7. They did a segment called "Star of the Week" every Friday night that featured an amateur athlete in Calgary who had done something exceptional, and they wanted to interview me! I couldn't believe it.

A moustachioed reporter named Ron Manz came to talk to me and Kelly at the gym, and a cameraman filmed us working together. When Ron asked me what my goal was, I rolled my eyes and said, "To go to the Olympics and win."

This was a surprise to Kelly. "When I saw him say that, I thought, 'oh, he's so precious; I'm not going to let that dream die.' It was cute," he recalled years later. "At the same time, I thought, boy, that was a silly thing to say. An Olympic gold medal—Jesus! But I just let it go, and we kept training."

Kelly knew a lot better than I did how unlikely it was that the two of us would one day be competing on an Olympic floor, let alone stand on top of the Olympic podium. But he remembered what it was like to be a kid with a dream, and he didn't dismiss the idea. He just kept quiet, and I kept dreaming.

· · ·

When I wasn't competing, I was watching more intensely. I never missed the opportunity to catch gymnastics on TV. I pored over the TV Guide each week and parked myself in front of the box half an hour before every televised competition began. In my hand I held the VCR remote, finger poised over the record button, ready to chop out the commercials. To my inner perfectionist, it was not acceptable that my beloved gymnastics tapes be cluttered with unimportant commercials.

I watched those elite competitions over and over, trying to pinpoint what made those athletes so good. I wanted to know everything about them: what time they got up in the morning and when they went to bed, what their days were like and how many floor routines they did at each practice. A subscription to *International Gymnast Magazine* fed my curiosity. I would tear it open and read it cover to cover the day it arrived. At the library, I checked out every book I could get my hands on about the sport. I discovered that gymnastics had so many larger-than-life figures, like the great Nadia Comaneci, who stunned the world by scoring seven perfect 10s at the 1976 Olympics in Montreal.

That same year, a Japanese man called Shun Fujimoto made an enormous sacrifice to assure his team won the gold medal. Japan had won four Olympic titles in a row and was gunning for a fifth. In the team final, Fujimoto broke his knee performing on floor exercise. He should have sat out the rest, but the team needed him to do rings in order to beat the Soviets.

Fujimoto got up, gritted his teeth, and did his exercise, dismounting from eight feet up onto his broken knee. Yowza. He betrayed just a small grimace of pain before bowing to the judges and hobbling off the mat. He would limp for the rest of his life, but his team got their gold. That was the magic of the Olympics, I thought. It was about surpassing whatever you thought was possible.

• • •

By this time, gymnastics was firmly settled at the centre of my life. I was totally obsessed; gymnastics was all I thought about and all I talked about. In school, I sat and daydreamed about the skills I was working on and would often surprise my teachers with a casual back handspring in the middle of gym class. At home after practice, I watched a growing stack of taped TV competitions over and over. As I drifted off to sleep, I pictured myself competing at the Olympic Games.

Kelly recognized this passion and did everything he could to fuel it. His responsibility, as he saw it, was to make training a balance between hard work and fun. He realized that if all we did was condition and repeat our skills a hundred times at every practice, we would lose our love for the sport. So he did everything he could to make the gym our home. We often did fun activities with the women's team, and soon my teammates became like family; in fact, we spent more time together in the gym than we did with our own siblings and parents. If we worked particularly hard as a group one day, Kelly would set up a ladder for us to climb and hang from the rafters for a thrilling thirty-foot drop into the foam pit. We were often rewarded with extra trampoline time to play around and improve our aerial awareness. In the summers we would all play epic games of Kick the Can in the dark.

Gymnastics, especially at a young age, is all about progressions and drills. Kelly was constantly seeking knowledge from other coaches like Tony and Eugene. He was always dreaming up new ways to help us break through on challenging skills. He was also willing to spot us a thousand times until we felt comfortable enough to try a difficult skill on our own. If we ever expressed any doubt about our ability to execute a certain skill, Kelly would tell us, "I would never say that you're ready unless I really believe that you can do it."

He also kept us motivated. Along with his charts on the wall, Eugene encouraged Kelly to have us track the number of elements we performed in a week. Kelly armed each of us with a binder full of blank pages and we made a tick for each skill we executed successfully. He wanted us to be able to look back and see the work we'd done. When given a task with a measurable component, I was able to put my head down and grind it out harder than anyone. I once performed thirty-seven vaults in a single practice. We had only been assigned ten, but I derived great satisfaction in exceeding Kelly's expectations and also in lapping my teammates.

Kelly understood that a coach's job is to guide, not criticize. Though perfect is always the gold standard, he knew we would be happier if we heard about the things we needed to do to make our skills and routines great rather than all the things we were doing wrong. He focused on the positive, and by doing so, he helped us avoid the negative. "Flowers grow better with water than they do with fertilizer," he often said.

. . .

In 1992, Altadore Gymnastics produced its very own Olympian. Jennifer Wood was the hardest worker I knew. I used to sneak little glimpses of her out of the corner of my eye in the gym. Jennifer was tiny and strong and had a special aura around her. Vault was her forte and she herself had scored a perfect 10 on this apparatus at the Altadore Invitational one year. It made her a thing of legend amongst my circle of nine-year-old superfans.

Jennifer's Olympics came after a career of almosts. She *almost* made the Olympic team in 1988. She *almost* made the Canadian World Championships teams in 1989 and 1991. In 1992, she finally got her break: she earned a spot on the Barcelona Olympic team, the first gymnast from Alberta to do so.

Everyone at the gym did something to help Jenn prepare for the Games. The coaches gave corrections and pep talks. A choreographer came in a few times a week to work with her. We younger gymnasts tripped over ourselves to get out of her way when we saw her coming.

Mostly though, we stared. To prepare for the biggest competition of her life, Jenn did pressure sets—routines in front of large crowds to replicate the competition atmosphere. Everyone in the gym clustered around the balance beam or the floor exercise to watch as she performed. The idea was to create that Olympic feel of performing before the world, where every eye is trained on you.

Jenn was my role model in the gym, though I was much too shy to tell her that. I was scared even to approach her. Once, we did a photoshoot together for the local paper and I could barely look at her in the eye. She was Jennifer Wood, Olympian, and I was Kyle Shewfelt, little boy with neatly slicked hair. Nevertheless, seeing Jenn pop up on the TV screen doing her floor exercise at the Barcelona Olympics was one of the defining moments of my childhood.

We spent a few weeks that summer with my aunt and uncle in Minnedosa. The weather was beautiful, but I refused to go outside. I sat glued to the living room TV and watched the Barcelona Olympics. Every single minute was captivating.

At my insistence, Mom brought an armful of VHS tapes on the trip. As usual, I either sat or held a headstand directly in front of the TV with the remote in my hand. When Jenn came on, I exclaimed, "I know her! She goes to *my* gym!" It gave me an immense amount of joy to be associated with someone competing in the Olympics.

The gym had a big celebration when Jenn returned from Barcelona. We all got a copy of her Canadian Olympic Team trading card, and she gave everyone a little coin from Spain. Twelve years later, stuffed in a pocket of my gym bag, those mementoes accompanied me to Athens for the 2004 Games.

Another athlete in Barcelona who inspired me tremendously was Canadian swimmer Mark Tewksbury, the gold medallist in the 100-metre backstroke. I'll never forget Mark thrashing the water in triumph after he touched the wall in first place. What really resonated about Mark's story was that he was born and raised in Calgary—a boy who had followed his dream to become an Olympic champion.

Jenn and Mark's Olympic experiences were a turning point for me. Somewhere deep inside my mind, a goal had been planted. Watching them compete in Barcelona showed me what I could accomplish. If someone from my city, who trained at my gymnastics club, could make it to the Olympic Games, why couldn't I? If someone from Calgary had won an Olympic gold medal, why couldn't I?

4

TRYING ON BAD

I DIDN'T EXPECT TO BE IN HANDCUFFS, BUT THERE I was. My crime was pocketing a yellow lighter with a marijuana plant on it from a store called San Francisco at the local mall. A mall security officer intercepted me a few steps after exiting the store and, grabbing my hood, frog-marched me to their offices, passing every table in the food court on the way. The perp walk was mortifying, but it didn't compare to when Mom arrived twenty minutes later and lost her mind.

"What the f--- are you doing with your life?" she erupted, her voice an octave higher at the possibility of a criminal in the family. Her angry alter ego was known as "the Wrath of Nola" in our family, and on this occasion, she unleashed it on me full force. "Your father and I are so disappointed in your behaviour lately. Stealing?! Kyle, when did you start stealing? You know that's not right. I didn't raise you this way." She put her hand on her forehead, her eyes bugging out of her head.

"I'm not stupid, you know," she continued. "I know what you've been up to. I know about the drinking. I know about the smoking. I know about the sneaking out at night."

She looked at the security guards. "You guys should just arrest him," she snapped.

"Would you like him to spend some time in a cell, ma'am?" one of them asked courteously.

"No, I've got him from here," she snarled, grabbing me hard by my collar. "You think you're so cool? You want to be a badass?" She turned me in the direction of the door and hauled me to the car, politely thanking the security team on the way out. I think even the guards were a little scared of her.

By the time I reached seventh grade, the strain of trying to be the perfect straight-A student and athlete was showing. I thought the world would grind to a halt if I put less than 100 percent effort into every single one of my tasks, from brushing my teeth to doing my math homework to achieving the perfect toe point on my double twist on floor. I was distraught when my overall report card average was 96.6 percent and I only ranked third on the honour roll. It was just unacceptable that I was not number one.

My unbelievably high expectations for myself came to a head when we were assigned a poetry project in English class and I didn't get it done on time. When the teacher asked what had happened, I broke down and started sobbing as I explained that I just hadn't had enough time to do it as well as I wanted. The word "FAILURE" flashed on and off like a lighted sign in my mind. The obsessive perfectionist living inside me—whose hair had to be perfectly slicked to the side, whose shirt was always perfectly tucked in, who had to be the very best at everything—had begun to impact my ability to function normally.

To make matters worse, my pubescent body seemed to have turned against me in the gym.

Here are a few discoveries one makes as a teenage boy in gymnastics:

One: there's a musky stench that begins emitting from your armpits. It's there every time you train pommel horse or parallel bars or just lift up your arms. Note that a gymnast spends about half his time with his arms over his head.

Two: gymnastics is about repetition and you realize that twenty hours a week is a huge amount of time to spend doing the same skills over and over again. It's even more frustrating when you fall or can't complete routines well 90 percent of that time. That's more than eighteen hours a week feeling like you're terrible at something.

Three: skills can be lost. Handstands become frustrating when you're growing and your centre of gravity is in constant flux. Skills that are fun and easy one day suddenly become impossible the next.

While your body is busy betraying you, things are not so great in your head, either. From the time I entered middle school, I was made fun of for being a boy who did gymnastics. Fag, homo, queer, fairy, pansy—in a single typical day at school, I heard them all. It didn't help that I was a head shorter than a lot of my classmates and had been a part of the Gifted and Talented Education Program, a.k.a. "Smart School" at Queen Elizabeth High since fifth grade.

"Why do you do gyyyyymmmmnaaaaasssstics?" was a common question, the word dragged out to make it sound ridiculous and lispy.

I also frequently got: "Nice shorts you wear," "Isn't that a sport for chicks?" and the old classic, "Doesn't doing the splits hurt your balls?"

Fortunately, I had a core group of friends who never made fun of me for my choice of sport or for being part of the smart-kids program. For every clown who thought he was macho for observing that *he* didn't run around in spandex in *his* sport, there were several truly supportive people who found it cool that I could grab a door frame with my fingertips and swing into a backflip. They respected how I got to travel and represent my province—and later my country—and they got to know just how hard I worked for the privilege. Many of these people are still my friends today.

Nevertheless, a rebellion was in the making.

The year I turned thirteen was the year I became a public terror. I dumped vanilla milkshakes into public mailboxes for fun. I lit paper towel dispensers on fire in the school bathroom. I discovered that smoking catnip—yes, *catnip*—from a pop-can bong kind of gets you high. I learned that if you microwave Magic Markers for ten seconds, the ink sprays out at least two feet in all directions when you remove the cap. My mom didn't know the full extent of what I was doing, but she knew enough to reach out for help.

• • •

"So," Dr. Hap Davis said, settling into his office chair, "tell me about you."

I sat in a plush green leather chair in Dr. Davis's office and looked around. The branches of the plant that stood next to the chair dangled down and tickled the top of my head. Dr. Davis, a sports psychologist, sat beside his grandfather's century-old Chippendale desk covered in piles of papers, with two big bookshelves behind him. He crossed his legs and leaned his chin onto his hand, looking at me intently. He had a tall, lean runner's build and wore light-framed glasses. In his eyes I detected gentleness. It was comforting. "Why don't you call me Hap?" he said.

Hap listened patiently as I explained why I felt I needed to be perfect all the time and the problems it was causing. "Is the world going to end if it's not perfect?" he asked. He spun in his chair, then stood up and began pacing around his office, gently rubbing his eyebrow with his hand, moving it up to the edge of a slightly receding hairline. He seemed to be mulling over the question. "Is the world going to end if it's not perfect?"

"No," I said. Realization dawned on me. Suddenly that seemed obvious. "No, I guess it won't."

"Ah!" Hap said, turning and pointing his finger at me like we'd just made a scientific discovery. "That landed." He sat back down beside his desk, folded his hands, and leaned forward again. "I work with a lot of athletes," he said, "and I can tell you that it's totally normal to feel the way you do. A lot of perfectionists feel that way. But it's important to remember that the world is not going to end if things aren't completely perfect."

"Yes," I said. The more I thought about it, the more it made sense.

Hap stood up, adjusted his glasses and resumed pacing. "So . . . what can we do about this? What do *you* think we should do about this?"

Together, we created a new mantra. From that day on, a poster with the words "THE WORLD WILL NOT END IF IT'S NOT PERFECT" hung on the wall above my bed.

Gradually, I came around to the idea that things didn't have to be perfect. In fact, I began wondering what would happen if I stopped giving a crap entirely. Come to think of it, I was sick of being the good student and sick of fighting my stupid, uncooperative body in the gym. The world could go to hell, I decided.

So I dyed my hair. I shot spitballs at the walls. I mouthed off to authority figures. I started being disrespectful to teammates I decided were no longer cool. One night, Scott took me to a party where I got wasted on peppermint schnapps and spent the evening hunched over the toilet puking my guts up. One of our friends ended up calling Mom to come and get me. "He's putting a buzzkill in the party here," I heard her saying matter-of-factly into the phone. Mom came and got me all right, then forced me to go to training the next day.

"I just wanted to let you know that Kyle got very drunk last night and didn't want to come this morning, but I dragged him out of bed, so he's here," she informed Kelly cheerfully.

"I'm so glad you're here, Kyle," Kelly said, equally cheerfully, smiling at Mom. "We've got a lot of conditioning in our plan today, just what you like. You can start with the shuttle runs . . ."

I was surly with my parents, who were spending their time driving across the city several days a week to shuttle me from school to practice and back to Dover. Once, Dad brought me a meatball sub so I'd have something to eat before training. He wasn't sure exactly what toppings I'd like, so his choices included lettuce. I unwrapped it. "Do you put lettuce on your spaghetti?" I commented acidly as I picked off each soggy strand one by one and flung them to the side. How Dad didn't pull over right there and make me walk the rest of the way, I'll never really understand.

I also decided that smoking was cool. I smoked across the street from the school with some of my friends, and sometimes in my bedroom, holding the cigarette out the window between puffs. I was engaged in this one night when Dad walked in and caught me just as I was lifting the cigarette to my lips. I swallowed the smoke, plucked the cigarette out of my mouth and held it behind my back. Smoke wafted upwards.

"Are you smoking?" Dad asked accusingly.

"No," I said in a nasal voice, trying not to breathe out. Strands of smoke curled over my head.

Dad made me use my savings to pay my gymnastics training fees that month. "If you're going to smoke, I'm not paying for your training," he said. "If you're going to make stupid, unhealthy choices, why should I invest in it? You can pay for it yourself." Bye-bye $350 . . . it was nice knowing ya!

• • •

Around 2 a.m., the wooden door of the Kingshead Pub swung open and Jody, one of the coaches at Altadore, stepped out. Her eyes widened in disbelief as she took in the four of us standing on the sidewalk, all looking in different directions to avoid making eye contact with her.

It was me and a couple of my teammates that night. Saturday morning practice began in exactly seven hours, but there we were, hoping to find someone who could score us alcohol from the liquor store across the street.

The scheme worked like this: we would all arrange to sleep over at one of our teammates' houses. Once his parents went to bed, we'd wait an hour and tiptoe out. We'd lurk on a street corner outside the pub, and eventually someone would come along drunk enough to accept $20 in exchange for buying us a bottle of vodka or a case of beer. We weren't picky, we just wanted to get buzzed.

Jody wasn't taken in for a second. "What in the hell are you guys doing out here in the middle of the night?" she screeched. "Do your mothers know where you are? Get out of here before you get hurt!"

We scattered like burglars who had just tripped the alarm to the bank vault. "And don't even think I'm going to hide this from Kelly!" Jody called after us. "I'm calling him first thing tomorrow morning!"

When we walked into the gym the next morning, Kelly was seething. In a tight-lipped, fatherly way, he lined us up and laid into us. He was very disappointed. He expected us to act professionally, make good choices and rest well the night before training. "Thirteen and outside a bar at 2 a.m.—what were you thinking?" he asked, his voice louder than usual. If staying up late, galivanting around the neighbourhood, and getting drunk the night before training was the choice we wanted to make, that was fine, but we would suffer the consequences. He would only put as much effort into coaching us as we would put into being first-class athletes. Which, at the moment, wasn't much.

Tired of bullies and angry at my body, I reached a point where my rebellious streak was ready to question *all* authority, even in the gym. Since I was six years old, Kelly had had 95 percent control over my training program. My job was to show up and execute the prescribed plan—until, with my brilliant teenage wisdom, I decided I didn't like having someone tell me what to do. I thought I knew the right way to do everything and was open to exactly zero suggestions. So I stopped listening and started talking back.

"Why are you showing up to the gym at all?" Kelly asked me one day. *Why do you do gyyyyymmmmnaaaaassssstics?* ran through my head.

I didn't know anymore. I wasn't having fun. I wasn't feeling progress. That week I showed up with my newfound snarky manner and zero incentive to train. Kelly had made a group plan that involved lots of strength and conditioning work. I whined loudly about the workload. After putting up with it for months, Kelly had heard enough.

"If you don't like it, you don't have to do it," he told me. "Get out."

I had never been thrown out of the gym; I was the team perfectionist, after all. Only a couple years before, Kelly almost had to forcibly pull me off the equipment at the end of a practice. But I was fed up. Screw Kelly, I thought. Screw everything. I was sick of training, sick of looking at Kelly's face, sick of being perfect little gymnast boy.

That night I told my parents I was done with gymnastics. From here on out, I proclaimed, I wanted to be a normal thirteen-year-old and just spend my time with my friends after school. Perhaps deep down I wanted to be talked out of this idea but, if so, I'd chosen the wrong person to vent to. The Wrath of

Nola came out again. As I opened my mouth to tell her for the umpteenth time what a jerk Kelly was, she cut me off.

"If you want to quit, that's fine," she said abruptly. "Go ahead. See how great life is when you're hanging out at 7-11 with your friends. It's not all it's cracked up to be, but if that's your choice, go ahead and be a loser. I'm done trying to convince you otherwise."

And that was the way it was. For a week.

Not that I admitted it, but I felt lost on Monday afternoon when I wasn't heading off to the gym. Instead, I rode the yellow school bus home with my friends and spent the evening watching TV and talking on the phone. Part of me wanted to go outside and jump on the trampoline, but I wasn't going to give in so easily.

By Wednesday, I was like a caged animal, doing handstands in the living room, as restless as I had been when I was six. Seriously, what did everybody do with their spare time? I hated to face it, but I was bored out of my tree. Two days later, I decided that I would go crazy if I didn't go back to the gym. On Monday, the new life philosophy had been "screw gymnastics." By Friday it was "screw normality, I want to be a gymnast again."

Some things did need to change, though. I wanted more independence and a greater say in my training plans, but I didn't know how to say that to Kelly. Finally my mom set up a meeting and we sat down with him. The Wrath of Nola got us started. "You two need to figure out a way to communicate more effectively with each other and work together," she said. "Kyle wants independence and Kelly wants authority. You both need to respect that and meet somewhere in the middle. You've worked together for so long and you are a great team when things are going well, but you are both unbearable and stubborn when things aren't going the way you want them to.

"Kyle, your father and I support you and your dream of becoming an Olympian. But I am through being put in the middle of your disagreements with each other. From this point forward, what happens at the gym is your business and I don't want to hear about it. Okay?"

"Okay," I muttered.

After that, Kelly said his piece about how I needed to come into the gym with a better attitude, ready to work. He talked about setting an example for the younger boys. "You need to choose the positive path and commit to your dream," he said. "If we can just get through this rough period—believe me, Kyle, I know what I'm talking about—the sky will be the limit.

"You have so much potential. These are going to be the hardest few years for you. If you can just keep yourself motivated and in shape through this time, you are going to be a phenomenal gymnast when you hit your late teens and beyond. The work will make you better. I don't want anything except to see you become the best gymnast you can possibly be. Remember when you were nine and you said you wanted to go to the Olympics and win? Don't let that dream disappear."

Good intentions can be misinterpreted as control when you're a teenager who wants to attack all things authority. In that moment, I saw that Kelly wasn't in this to make my life hell. He wanted to see me succeed. "I've seen so many young boys who were so good never make it to the senior level," Kelly said. "That is my whole goal, to get you to stay in it, to be in the sport when you are a man, not a boy, so that you can make your decisions as a man."

I felt nervous when it was my turn to speak. I had never had the platform to express what I needed before. After stumbling for words and staring at the floor, I said that I wanted to feel more independent in my training. To my surprise, Kelly agreed. He was going to let me have more independence in the gym. In fact, he was going to let every boy at Altadore have more of a say in their training plans. The first qualifier for the Canadian Championships was two months away. Kelly proposed an experiment: this time, we would be entirely in charge of our own preparation. Enthusiastically, I agreed.

Kelly always pushed me to do more conditioning to compensate for my skinny arms and relative lack of upper-body strength, which was important for events like rings and pommel horse. But I didn't like doing rope climbs, so I shrugged them off. The whole team conditioned lazily.

To say that we bombed that meet is an understatement. I fell off the pommel horse four times. The rings swung out of control during my dislocate sequence. On floor, my toes touched the floor on a press handstand because I didn't have the stamina to lift them up at the end of the routine.

As the meet wore on, I became ashamed at raising my arm to signal that I was ready to compete. I didn't feel ready at all. Other coaches stood with crossed arms and shook their heads. In a word, the whole thing was a disaster.

When it was all over, Kelly called a team meeting. We lined up side by side while Kelly stood in front of us with condolences in his eyes but a heady grin on his face. "So guys, how do you think it went?" he asked, arching his eyebrows.

We hung our heads in shame.

"Are you ready to try a different approach and build a plan *together*?"

We nodded meekly.

"Good. I'll see you at training Monday afternoon. 4 p.m. sharp. Let's get back on track and kick some butt at nationals."

A different coach might have rubbed our faces in it, but Kelly realized the sting of this loss would stay with us because we had done it to ourselves. It must have been painful for him to watch the buildup and to see that carnage on the mats, but in order for us to realize the importance of a collaborative effort, he had to let us fail. It's a lesson I never forgot.

5

THE ELITE WORLD

THE JACKET WAS WHITE, WITH ONE RED SLEEVE
and maple leaves embroidered on the front and on one of the
arms. It came with white shorts, long pants with stirrup bottoms,
and a crimson singlet that had a white maple leaf dead in the
centre of the chest. My first national team uniform had arrived
in the mail in a puffy brown envelope that afternoon and my
heart was thumping with happiness.

I wore it around the house all night. Several times I went
to the bathroom mirror and looked over my shoulder to see
the word "CANADA" embroidered across the back. This was a
monumental occasion, definitely worthy of the hallway fashion
show and awkward picture taken by my proud mom.

With the worst of my teenage rebellion behind me, Kelly and
I regained some balance. I was competing in the tyro category
at that point—one below novice, followed by junior and then
senior. Only seniors were eligible to compete on World and
Olympic teams. I buckled down in training and went on to win
the 1996 Canadian Championships in my age category, edging
out Ken Ikeda, a super talented boy from British Columbia. My

margin of victory was a mere 0.05, meaning a tiny execution error like a bent knee or an unpointed toe would have reversed the standings.

Later that summer, Ken and I and a handful of fourteen- to sixteen-year-old boys from across the nation were selected to compete at two international invitational meets in Austria and Hungary that fall. They would be our first assignments representing our country, not just our clubs or provinces. I couldn't wait. I was curious to see how I stacked up against the rest of the world.

What I didn't know was that my parents had taken out a line of credit to finance this opportunity for me. Gymnastics was my life, but it had taken over part of theirs as well. They partook in fundraisers, selling cookie dough and raffle tickets and working bingo nights to make sure the gym kept its doors open. The club was not privately owned; it was a not-for-profit society run by a volunteer group of parents who sat as its board of directors. Mom took on the role of president for a couple of years. Dad was at every gym meet equipment setup. Quietly, always manoeuvring in the background, they had begun putting in their own time and making sacrifices to give me the chance to succeed.

• • •

1996 was an Olympic summer and, as usual, I spent it glued to the TV drinking in all the action from Atlanta's Georgia Dome. Unlike in previous years, I watched the competition with an appraising eye. Seeing the gymnasts tumble across the screen and comparing what they were doing with the things I was working on, I felt the Olympic dream shift slightly and move just a bit closer. I was fourteen and not at their level yet, but watching the Games helped me become more confident that one day I might be.

Along with the electrifying performances of the American women's team, one gymnast stood out over all the others that year. Men's all-around silver medallist Alexei Nemov of Russia had a special flair and elegance, especially on floor exercise. His tumbling was first class, but he also had incredible charisma. And toe point. By the end of the Games, where he pocketed five medals, Nemov was my new idol. More than any other, he was the gymnast I wanted to be like.

. . .

I had imagined that travelling the world as a gymnast meant staying in first-class hotels with swimming pools and room service, and executing routines in pristine, brightly lit arenas packed with screaming fans. The reality proved quite different.

We moved in a straggly line toward the city bus stop, dragging our rolling suitcases over the muddy cobblestone streets of Vienna. Our group stayed in one-star hostels, where we slept in one large room furnished with several bunk beds. Cracks ran down the cream-coloured walls. Every morning, we trudged down to the dining room to eat buns with meat and cheese before boarding the bus to a training gym thirty minutes away.

The gym, too, was a far cry from the glamorous competition venues I imagined. The floor we tumbled on must have been twenty years old. It was a dull golden colour and filled with dead spots—places where the floor springs had worn out. You could hurt your ankles or back hitting a dead spot, so we took hunks of chalk and circled places to avoid.

Despite all that, the quality of the gymnastics shown was a real eye-opener. The rest of the world was much better than we were, I discovered. The other boys there, mostly from Central and Eastern Europe, trained far more intensely than we did. For every tumbling pass we did in training, they did three. Often they casually nudged us out of the way in lines to use the apparatus, sending the message that our presence was wildly inconvenient. They conditioned like well-oiled machines, grinding out handstand push-ups and doing vertical leaps as high as their chests. In competition, they executed more difficult tricks with stellar precision and fought not to give away deductions as though their lives depended on it. Watching them, I was reminded of soldiers training for war. Comparatively, we looked like total amateurs—and they probably would have agreed.

From Vienna we took a train to Kiskunhalas, Hungary, for the Hungarian Youth Invitational. Our favourite part of that competition was the clown at the end, who entertained the crowd with a comedic parallel bars routine while results were tabulated. The clown had us all in stitches as he kept falling on his groin between the bars, pretending to be clumsy. For his big finale, he did a dismount that he managed to land straddling one bar. His animated facial expressions, eyes and mouth wide open in perpetual surprise, made us laugh so hard we cried.

After the show, the clown came bouncing up to us. "Canadians!" he exclaimed. "Hello! I am Uldi and I like to speak English. Maybe I can practice with you?"

Uldi's full name was Zoltan Miklos Hajdu. Out of his clown makeup, he had movie-star looks and a wide, friendly smile. It turned out he had been on the Hungarian national team for several years. He was friendly with everyone, and he and Kelly really hit it off. Before the end of our trip, Kelly told him that he was welcome to help coach us in Canada. Uldi loved the idea and promised to try.

I ended up winning gold on vault and a bronze on floor in Hungary, which gave me hope for the future, but overall I felt embarrassed about my showing. Those European meets opened my eyes. It was very apparent that I needed to up my game if I wanted to be among the best in the world one day. *I'll train harder*, I promised myself.

• • •

As national champion in the tyro category, it was generally assumed that I would compete in the novice division in 1997, and I felt a lot of pressure to do so. Moving up was the logical thing to do, but I just didn't feel ready. I was still struggling and adjusting to my growing body. My centre of gravity changed every week and my self-confidence fluctuated from hour to hour. The novice category also had compulsory routines that were extremely challenging for me on some events because of my toothpick arms. The Sydney Olympics were three years away, but at the beginning of 1997 the goal had never seemed more out of reach.

Kelly stepped in. Since we were all spending more than twenty hours a week sweating and falling and pushing our comfort zones, it was important to him that we felt a sense of accomplishment about it all. Kelly understood that if you can get through the difficult adolescent period, all of your skills will eventually come back, you'll start to build muscle, and gymnastics will become fun again. It was only a matter of time.

Together, we decided that I would spend another year in the tyro division. "I'd rather you win tyro again and feel like you did great and that all of your dedication is worth it, than finish twentieth in novice and feel like a failure," Kelly told me. We decided that the goal for the 1997 Canadian Championships in Ottawa, Ontario was to hold my chin up high and maximize the quality of my work.

Not everyone agreed with Kelly. Ken and several boys who had finished behind me in 1996 had moved up to novice, and some coaches asked why I didn't just suck it up and try it for a year. "What should I do when people question why I'm still in tyro?" I asked, anticipating more uncomfortable conversations.

"You tell them you didn't feel ready to move up and that it was *our* decision," Kelly said firmly. "Listen to me, Kyle: when it comes to your own life, you are always right. No one knows what's right for you more than you. Let people say what they want. And if they have any other questions, they can come and talk to *me*."

I won my second tyro national all-around title that year, in a convincing victory, and left Ottawa feeling confident we had made the right choice. In the months to come, Kelly and I came to another conclusion: in 1998, I would compete as a junior, skipping the novice category entirely.

We never heard a word of criticism about the decision again.

· · ·

Despite my newfound determination to train harder than ever, it was easier said than done. Adapting to co-pilot roles with Kelly wasn't always easy and my unpredictable teenage moods didn't make the process any smoother. We would work well for several months, then hit another rough patch. We were going through one such phase when Uldi, the Hungarian groin-crushing gymnastics clown, appeared at the gym, suitcase and work visa in hand, for a stint as Kelly's assistant coach.

"Kyle, in the plan today you've got five rope climbs," Kelly said a few days later.

I groaned. Rope climbs were still high on my list of least favourite things. "Ugh, I'm so tired," I whined. "Can't I do something else?" Kelly shook his head, exasperated. "You know what would be great? If I didn't have to light a fire under your a-- all the time to get you to do something," he fumed.

Uldi, somewhere between Kelly and me in age, silently took in this exchange, looking first at Kelly then turning to me. "Come on Kyle, let's go," he said, waving me over. "He's just looking out for you. Let's get it done." He shook his shaggy brown hair out of his eyes, then grabbed one of the ropes and began shimmying up. Knowing I'd look like an idiot if I stood there and continued arguing, I grabbed the other rope and did what Kelly had asked. From then on, Uldi assumed a unique role: half coach, half training partner.

Training with Uldi made things a lot more fun. He was always in a good mood, and he injected a new element of energy and creativity into the training sessions. And since I couldn't push his buttons the way I could push Kelly's, I listened to him.

Uldi was extremely strong and could still hold his own in the gym. He was especially good on rings, my worst event.

Occasionally he would grip up and do the same workout I had been assigned, and usually he kicked my butt. Uldi could hold an iron cross easily for thirty seconds, while I could barely hold it for two. It's hard to talk back to someone who schools you on the skills you're struggling to do, so I listened, and little by little, I got better.

Uldi swore by something he called "the Gauntlet." The Gauntlet consisted of doing bicep curls with thirty-pound dumbbells until you were exhausted, then switching them out for twenty-five-pound dumbbells, then twenty, fifteen, ten, five, and finally two. By the time we were done, I was barely able to lift the two-pound weights, but my arms looked double their size, or so Uldi claimed.

As a finishing touch, Uldi always made me flex my muscles for an entire minute standing in front of the gym mirror to "lock in the power," as he put it.

"It's for your own good," he added with his sly grin. "You need to get stronger, not just for gymnastics, but also for the ladies." I shrugged and complied. Since every mom at the gym got googly eyed when Uldi walked by, I figured he must have known what he was talking about.

Uldi helped my muscles and confidence grow. With his motivation and influence, I would soon be needing a larger-sized Team Canada outfit.

6

BULLY

AS MY CAREER BEGAN TAKING OFF, KELLY AND I were invited to self-funded training camps across the country, and also began travelling farther afield for competitions. Although I was having a great time, by Grade 9 balancing school, training, and travelling was a problem. I took my textbooks with me on the road but didn't often open them. The mad panic of trying to get caught up when I got back always left me feeling stressed out and drained.

Scott Lang, a friend who trained at the U of C, offered a solution. Calgary has something called the National Sport School (NSS), which makes accommodations for promising student athletes struggling to balance high school with high-level training and travel.

"It's awesome," Scott proclaimed. "You pretty much get to design your own schedule, and the teachers are flexible with homework deadlines and testing dates." The idea appealed to me, and though it would be a daily commute of about thirty minutes each way, my parents and I decided to give it a try.

Scott was right: the NSS turned out to be a great fit for my needs. I was able to arrange school around my training and travel, which allowed me to have some incredible experiences. After I finished second at the 1998 nationals as a junior, I was selected to go to the World Youth Games in Russia, where, against many of the top juniors on the planet, I won a silver medal on floor and placed fourth on vault.

Before the Games, we trained at the famous Dynamo Gymnastics Club in Moscow, where history seeped from the rafters. The atmosphere inside the gym was intense but I got a special feeling thinking that many of the sport's greatest stars had trained on the same equipment and bickered with their coaches under the same roof.

Occasionally we spotted celebrities. We were stretching one day when Svetlana Khorkina, the reigning world champion in women's gymnastics, floated regally through the gym, carrying a brown paper bag from McDonald's. I could smell the french fries as she passed. We all kept our eyes firmly glued to the mat in front of us, fearful that this queenlike creature would catch us staring.

High on that experience, I returned to the NSS in September ready for another excellent school year. And I would have had it too, had it not been for that bully.

. . .

"Hey fag."

He was bigger than I was, and stronger than I was, and when I think of him now, he reminds me of a dog who smelled fear. Whenever I walked by, he picked up the scent and then he was on me.

By the time I was in eleventh grade, I had gotten used to the teasing that came from being a boy in a "girly" sport. But the harassment I received this time was on a different level. The bully sensed that I was weaker than he was and used it against me. I was sixteen, fairly small and not inclined to fight anyway, and he knew I couldn't stand up to him.

This person did everything he could to make my life miserable. He would come up behind me at the beginning of English class and, with his lips close to my ear, say in that menacing whisper, "Hey faggot. Are you going to suck my d--- after school, you little queer gymnast? Would you like that?"

When he saw me coming down the hallway, he would start galloping on his tiptoes and flapping his arms like fairy wings while his buddies stood beside their lockers and laughed. I kept my eyes on the ground, determined not to acknowledge him. When he whispered to me before class, I cowered in my seat with my jaw set, staring straight ahead and pretending he didn't exist. Silently, I willed him to go away and leave me alone.

A few months of this made me afraid to go to school. I was always on my guard, trying to be invisible and wondering if he was lurking somewhere nearby. The fear became all-consuming. I felt anxious doing my homework, brushing my teeth, going to sleep at night. I began having trouble concentrating at the gym, too. As I swung around the high bar, my mind would be wandering, thinking about the next time he'd corner me and what he'd say or do. The gym was my sanctuary, and he got in my head even there.

To avoid the taunting, I started skipping class. I was now training twenty-four hours a week, doing two sessions per day. I had my driver's licence, which allowed me to come home after morning practice and hide out for the day while my parents and Scott were at work. Before going back to the gym in the afternoon, I'd make sure to clean up any evidence that I had been home.

All that time alone gave me plenty of opportunity to consider the situation. Maybe the bully was right, I thought. Maybe I should just quit. If I didn't do gymnastics, maybe I wouldn't be seen as an easy target. Maybe then he'd leave me alone.

. . .

"Is everything all right at school?" Mom asked evenly one night, looking deep into my eyes in that I'm-your-mother-and-I'm-worried-about-you way. Years later, I learned she had received a call from a concerned teacher because I hadn't been showing up to class. Additionally, the teacher reported, my behaviour had shifted. From being an engaged and enthusiastic student the year before, I was suddenly quiet and withdrawn. All of this was cause for concern, and the teacher had flagged it and reached out to my parents.

I hesitated. I was so ashamed of what was happening to me. My mind ran through the potential consequences of telling her what was really going on. What would the bully do if I ratted him out? Would he pants me in the middle of the hallway instead of just flying those "fairy wings"? Would he push me around in the locker room, or even worse, force to me do something sexual? Would he stand up in front of class when the teacher wasn't there and make me the butt of everyone's joke? The possibilities were endless. If he knew I snitched on him, he'd find a way to *really* make my life a living hell, I figured. I felt as if nothing I did was going to make him leave me alone.

So when Mom asked if anything was wrong, I gave a tight-lipped response. I never told anyone—not my parents or my brother or Kelly or Hap or any of my friends—what was going on.

Instead of dealing with the issue, I devised a way out. That November, I lobbied my parents to let me complete my education by taking online and correspondence courses. Driving across the city to attend classes was a waste of time, I argued. Losing hours in the car made no sense when I could be studying via correspondence, getting a high school diploma and going to university afterward.

"If I'm going to be ready to make a run at the 2000 Olympics, this is the best thing for me and my training," I argued—convincingly, as it turned out. On some level, I was trying to convince myself, too. My parents accepted it as one more concession to gymnastics, along with sleeping in on Saturday mornings and going on real family vacations. As always, they let me make my own decision. I never told them the real reason was that I was tired of living in fear.

I'll never forget that bully and his taunts, nor how helpless I felt against them. These days I hear countless stories from parents whose children want to quit their sport or activity because of similar torments. If I could go back in time, I would muster up the courage to tell someone and ask for help. It's very hard when you're ashamed and paralyzed by fear, but it's an important step I didn't take. Sharing your struggle can foster a network of support and disrupt the pattern. Bullies thrive on fear, and having allies on your side can help extinguish their power. I wish I had understood that then.

In a way, that bully deepened my commitment to gymnastics. While I briefly considered dropping the sport, I also realized that giving up would be letting him win. At the same time, he also made me run away from a problem, something I will always wish I hadn't done.

I'll never make someone feel this way, I vowed as I cleaned out my locker on my last ever day of regular school. *And if ever I get the chance, I will go out of my way to stand up for those who are bullied because they don't fit the norm.* With a satisfying bang, the locker slammed shut. *In my world, they'll be accepted, included, and celebrated.*

I grabbed my bag and passed through the school doors for the final time. I was going to continue doing what made me happy. I was going to get vindication by achieving my goals. *I'll show you,* I thought. *I'll send you a postcard from the Olympics.* Not.

. . .

One of the big positives of my time at the NSS was that I got to take a sports psychology class. It came at a great time, because apart from dealing with the bully, my biggest struggle as a gymnast was staying motivated during the long months of training when there were no big competitions on the horizon.

I was blossoming, learning bigger and more difficult skills. My competition vault was a Yurchenko with a double twist, the same as many of the top seniors. I was even playing with adding an extra half twist at the end, making an already hard vault exponentially more difficult. Nobody else in the world was doing the Yurchenko with two and a half twists, and one of my goals was to be the first. Sports psych, with its goal-setting sheets, visualizations, relaxation techniques, and checklists for success, helped keep me on track.

I decided it would be a good idea to start capturing some of the visions swirling through my head. I knew what I wanted in gymnastics now, and it seemed like the moment to put some things down on paper. My goal sheet included the following:

I want to make a difference for Canadian gymnastics.
I want to invent a skill and have it named the Shewfelt.
I want to win a World Championships medal.
I want to become a world champion.
I want to be an Olympian.
I want to win the Olympic Games.

Once the list was made, I stuck it onto my bulletin board in my room so I would have to look at it every day.

This was not a daydreamer's list. It was 1998 and the Olympic Games were two years away. With the bully out of my life, my focus narrowed in.

7

TRY AND TRY AGAIN

"NO WAY AM I DOING THAT," I SAID.

It was 7:30 a.m. and Eugene, Uldi, and I were the only ones in the gym. We were in the middle of an early-morning training session with Eugene, who had accepted an offer to spend three months at Altadore. The club had received a grant and Kelly convinced the board to spend it on bringing Eugene in for a longer stint. He felt some significant time with Eugene would help everyone in the club evolve. Uldi referred to him as "Eugenius." There's nothing like a small Russian man in a red Adidas tracksuit and gymnastics shoes to bring a little business to the office.

Boosting my difficulty was a big part of the Eugenius agenda. I needed a spectacular skill to spice up my high bar routine, and Eugene had just the thing.

"No," I repeated. "Absolutely not."

Eugene fixed me with one of his unblinking stares. He could be like a thick stone wall: you can bang your head against it, but in the end it doesn't budge and you just end up with a big goose egg. His brilliant idea was to teach me a Def, a skill where the gymnast lets go of the bar, does a flip in a straight body position with one and a half twists, and then re-catches. It was invented by a French daredevil named Jacques Def, and like most high-level gymnastics skills, it is spectacular to watch and terrifying to think about doing.

Eugene finally convinced me to try the move from the high bar suspended over the big foam pit. Fine, I said. I swung out and launched myself about eight feet away from the bar to make sure that there was no chance I'd even come close to catching it. As I tapped out and twisted through the air, I had no clue where I was. Landing in the soft foam pit brought a keen sense of relief.

Eugene laughed. "Okay, first one out of the way," he said, his thick Russian accent still as nasally and prominent as it had been when I was nine. "Now do it again. Swing little higher, kick toes up more before release and bring closer."

We worked on it almost every day, sometimes twice a day, for the next three months. Eugene would stand beside the bar and give me technical corrections. I would swing into it and let go and Uldi would throw a mat over the bar as I flipped. That way I could bang my grips against the mat, getting a feel for the skill without worrying about actually catching the bar, or worse, smashing my face against it if I was too close. I liked all of my teeth where they were, thank you.

It was a team effort: Eugene advised, I flipped, Uldi threw the mat, over and over and over again.

Of all the skills I learned, the Def was the scariest of all. I did not believe in my ability to do it, let alone perform it consistently in competition. Eugene felt differently. When he was excited, Eugene talked with his hands to illustrate concepts that his

English wasn't quite fluent enough to convey. He did this a lot during that time.

"This skill made for you. You are good in air and you can swing," he explained, gesturing emphatically. "This skill, difficulty level is high and the crowd, they will love it. All you need is courage. And courage you can build, little by little. Be willing to try. Be open to learning."

Very, very slowly, I started to build courage. I'd always had catlike air sense, and after the first few attempts I understood intuitively where the bar was and how I'd need to position myself to catch it. Little by little, I kicked harder in the bottom of the swing and waited a nanosecond more before releasing my grip, inching the skill in closer. Finally, after twelve weeks of incremental progress, I kicked my toes up, released, did a flip with one and a half twists, and wrapped my hands around the bar. My grips clung. I'm still not sure how it happened. I was close enough, Uldi saw that I was safe and didn't throw the mat, and somehow I caught and stayed on.

Elated, Eugene came over and cupped my face with his hands, pinching my jowls like a baby's. Clapping and chuckling, he exclaimed, "See, I told you this skill made for you!"

Nothing compares to the feeling you get the first time you catch a complicated release move. Adrenalin courses through your entire body. You're simultaneously afraid for your life and in an aggressive, attack mindset. When you make the skill, you're surprised and ecstatic. Your knees turn to Jell-O, your hands shake and your heart thumps wildly in your chest. You can't wait to get back up and do it again.

And then you don't catch the next twenty. That's gymnastics for you.

Those months of training paid off: the Def became one of my most reliable skills. By the end of my career, I hadn't missed one in competition in more than five years, and in training, I caught 99 of every 100 I tried.

This is one of the more powerful lessons that sport taught me: success is never instantaneous. To get what you want, you have to show up and do the work. You have to keep on trying, even when it's frustrating and scary. Day after day, you have to put on your grips, do the drills and repetitions, make the small corrections. Eventually, it all comes together. Persistence pays off. Period.

. . .

In 1996 I was among the top five in Canada in my age group on everything except pommel horse. By 1998, I was top five only on floor, vault, and high bar. I wasn't built for rings, parallel bars or pommel horse—my long arms and strong legs were not an ideal combination for success on these events. On top of my physical limitations, I didn't enjoy training on these apparatus as much, which made it hard to master complicated moves. As a result, my scores on those events suffered, even though excellent marks on my best events kept me in the all-around conversation.

Boosted by my strengths, I closed out 1998 by winning the all-around title at Elite Canada in Burlington, Ontario. I had come a long way in just two years. Still, knowing the Sydney Olympics were just under two years away gave me a sinking feeling. I was doing well; a few had even begun talking about me as a top Canadian prospect for the 2004 Olympics in Athens. Athens was definitely the more realistic goal and Sydney was just the dream, but somehow I couldn't stop thinking about the dream.

Not long after that, Kelly and I decided I would try my chances in the senior level in 1999. It was early, and risky to do so: I would barely be seventeen. Even so, something told me it was the right thing to do.

. . .

My senior debut at the 1999 Canadian Championships in Burnaby, British Columbia could not have been better. The long hours of work Kelly, Eugene, Uldi, and I had devoted to my preparation paid off as I won the national title on floor exercise and debuted my new Yurchenko two and a half twist to add the title on vault. I also caught the Def for the first time in competition, which elicited loud cheers from the crowd, just as Eugene had predicted. Once again, lower scores on the other four events resulted in an eleventh-place all-around finish, well behind the top contenders. But it had also scored me an invitation to the World Championships team selection camp in Fredericton, New Brunswick, where we were all participating in an internal selection meet. And it wasn't going well.

I reached out, expecting to wrap my hands around the fibreglass rail. They closed around air. There was just enough time for a solitary thought—*uh-oh*—before my ribs crashed down on the parallel bars.

There's often an unpleasant half second when a skill goes wrong and you have just enough time to wonder how this is all going to end. In this case, my body folded itself in half over one parallel bar, where I dangled for a second before slumping onto the floor and staying there, trying to catch my breath. I felt close to tears. Here was a golden chance to make it to my first Worlds, and I was blowing it royally.

Unlike the national championships, trials for major teams were intimate, closed-door affairs. The 1999 Worlds were especially important because the top twelve teams qualified their countries to compete at the 2000 Olympic Games. The Olympics were the target every team was aiming for.

I stood up, took a few deep breaths, then got back up on the bars and finished my routine. Silence resounded through the gym as my feet hit the mat on my double pike dismount and I turned to bow to the judges. It wasn't enough. When the team for the World Championships was announced, my name wasn't called.

I was disappointed, but I understood. Though I could potentially post big numbers on floor and vault, I was young and inexperienced. The team relied on guys who could put up respectable scores on all six events. Even if I could deliver my best, any ground I picked up for the team was likely to be erased by my scores on my weaker events.

"Don't worry," Kelly said consolingly as I packed my bags to head back to Calgary. "This will be the last Worlds team you don't make."

• • •

Even though I didn't compete there, the 1999 World Championships in Tianjin, China shaped my Olympic destiny. The Canadian men finished a disappointing eighteenth as a team, dashing several Olympic dreams in the process. The upshot was that Canada would not be represented by a full team on the men's side at the Sydney Games. Eighteenth place did, however, earn Canada the opportunity to send two male gymnasts to Sydney.

Ironically, the result shifted the short-term priorities of the Canadian men's program. In the space of an afternoon, Gymnastics Canada, the national governing body for the sport, went from focusing on building a well-balanced team to taking a much closer look at potential individual event specialists.

From the beginning, one of those places was spoken for. By earning world silver on high bar in apparatus finals, Canada's first world medal in twelve years, Alexander "Sasha" Jeltkov, a fun-loving, rosy-cheeked Quebecois, all but cemented his Olympic spot. That left one place, and whether the Canadian Olympic Committee would even bother to use it was a mystery. The Olympic Committee quickly made it clear to Gymnastics Canada that it was not interested in sending an all-arounder to Sydney to finish around fiftieth place. The Olympic Committee wanted a guy who could potentially make a final—the top eight—in at least one event. World silver in his pocket, Sasha was covered. Anyone else would have to prove that they were worth the investment.

Hardy Fink, the men's technical director of Gymnastics Canada, stepped up with a question. "Suppose there is a gymnast who can manage to attain a top sixteen or better ranking on one or two events on the world cup circuit before the Games?" he asked the Olympic Committee. "Would you agree to send that gymnast to Sydney?" The Olympic Committee thought it over and agreed.

Victorious, Hardy went home and wrote down a short list of potential event specialists based on what he had seen at nationals and World trials. At the top of the list were two names: Richard Ikeda and my own.

8

THE OPPORTUNITY

YELENA PRODUNOVA, A PETITE, FEISTY RUSSIAN redhead composed almost entirely of muscle, handed the gas station attendant a 100 deutsche mark note and received a bottle of Baileys Irish Cream in return. She ripped off the seal and swiftly removed the cap. Smiling, she held the bottle out to me.

"You want to drink?" she asked.

"Da," I answered. Yelena was one of the great vaulters and tumblers in women's gymnastics. I loved the way she strutted around the gym like she owned it, attacking one apparatus after another. I may have tried on bad, but Yelena, with her eight-pack stomach, shaved eyebrow, and devil-may-care attitude, was the genuine article. I, on the other hand, freaked out if I went to bed without brushing my teeth. Yelena was the total opposite of me in every way and, to my surprise, we got along great. Yelena spoke decent English, and when she got tired of that she lapsed into Russian, which I pretended to understand.

I swigged happily at the bottle and passed it off to Alena Polozkova, a gymnast friend from Belarus. Then we went off to a disco to meet a group of other gymnasts to celebrate our

performances at the Cottbus World Cup in Germany. This was
not at all how I'd imagined trying to prove to the Canadian
Olympic Committee that I deserved to go to the Sydney
Olympics.

It was so, so much better.

· · ·

Everything was fresh and blooming in Montreux, Switzerland
in March 2000 as we headed to the first stop on the yearly world
cup circuit. Montreux is a ritzy resort town on Lake Geneva that
backs up to the Alps, but walking into its municipal gymnasium
was like stepping back in time. A thick cloud of chalk dust hung
over everything. The equipment, the same dull golden colour
it had been when I was a youngster in Austria, looked ancient.
A small but enthusiastic crowd of about five hundred filled the
gym to watch us compete.

My newcomer status didn't give me much street credit. Sasha
made me hold doors open for him wherever we went. "You're
the rookie, it's your job," he joked with a grin. As we walked
through the gym on the first day of training, I was exhilarated
but not confident enough to lift my eyes off the ground. I was
seventeen and didn't know if I belonged. This was a world I had
only imagined being a part of.

To give both Richard and me a fair shot at cracking the
world cup rankings on our best events, Gymnastics Canada had
decided to send us both to a minimum of three world cups. Kelly
and I figured that if I could place in the top eight on either floor
or vault at two of them, I would be able to earn enough points
to squeeze into the top sixteen in the overall rankings, meeting

the Canadian Olympic Committee's minimum requirement. Montreux was the first test.

While I was gaping at the equipment, Sasha was shaking hands with the other gymnasts, most of whom he already knew. I felt a pang of envy as I watched Sasha's confident smile and easy interactions, saluting people in Russian and French as easily as he did in English, every inch a member of this exclusive club. In my warm-up uniform, a pair of red track pants, an old sweatshirt, and a grey fleece zip-up vest several sizes too big, I felt like a total imposter.

As we walked onto the floor to begin stretching, a torrent of uncertainty flooded my brain. What if I wasn't good enough for this? What if I bombed so badly that I made a fool of myself in front of all these world-class gymnasts? The pressure felt so heavy that had I not glanced at Kelly, I might have turned around and run right out of the gym. Kelly too was gazing around, but there were stars in his eyes and a sizable grin plastered all over his face as he absorbed every ounce of the greatness surrounding us. I may have been afraid, but Kelly was just inspired.

We nodded at the Chinese team sitting and stretching by the high bar. The Japanese, wearing puffy silver coats with "JAPAN" inscribed in a flashy gold and red zigzag script, were engaged in their pre-competition ritual: lying spread-eagled on the floor and doing exactly nothing. What appeared to be laziness, I learned later, was actually strategy. Don't do too much before the competition, their theory went. You don't win medals in the warm-up.

The Russians, by contrast, were hard at work. They had jogged and stretched, and were currently occupying themselves conditioning, churning out press handstands and squat jumps in lines across the floor. Sasha went right up to them and started chatting. He shook hands with every single Russian gymnast and coach, saying what sounded like "Privyet, kak dela [hello, how are you?]" to each.

Trailing behind Richard, I shyly followed suit. Richard had earned the respect of the gymnastics community by competing at the 1996 Olympics and by making high bar finals at the World Championships the same year. He was looking to earn world cup ranking points on pommel horse and parallel bars, two of his strongest events. No one had ever seen me before. As I looked down the line that had formed to greet us, I recognized a familiar face. I had seen it on TV at the Olympics, and on the VHS replays of his floor exercise a thousand times.

It was Alexei Nemov. My favourite gymnast and idol, in the flesh.

Starstruck, I froze for an instant, afraid to shake his hand, because clearly I had not earned the right to touch such gymnastics royalty. I was just an inexperienced Canadian kid with big dreams who happened to be okay at tumbling. What the hell was I doing here?

But suddenly Alexei Nemov was in front of me, stretching out his hand and saying "privyet." I shook it firmly and repeated his greeting. Alexei was magnanimous and welcoming. It seemed to me that he understood how special a moment like this could be for a young Canadian kid. He made me feel like I had just arrived at a big show I had waited years to be a part of, and it made me idolize him even more.

The golden floor mat was kind to me, too. In my first-ever world cup, I finished a respectable seventh on floor and eleventh on vault.

One down, two to go. We headed to Cottbus, Germany.

. . .

"Von Ka-na-da . . . Ky-lie ZU-feld!"

That must be me, I giggled inwardly before stepping up to salute the head judge. The finalists at the 2000 Cottbus World Cup all got a big introduction before their routines. For the next seven years, whenever I competed in Germany, I would be introduced as "Kylie." It made me smile every time, wondering if this was how my mom's German-Czech ancestors would have pronounced it.

Many of the same gymnasts who had competed in Montreux also went to Cottbus, and seeing them again a week later was like meeting old friends. I now snuck in a wave to Yelena and the Russian girls when I passed them in the training gym. Yelena usually glared back like she wanted to put me in a headlock. Then, if her coach wasn't looking, she'd stick her tongue out at me.

The gymnasts on the circuit were all eager to hang out and most spoke near fluent English, which made me feel like a chump for not having a second language. "Where are you from?" was a common question. I would always say Canada, but people wanted a more specific response.

"No, but like, what are you?" they would ask.

In trying to emulate Nemov and working with Eugene, I had developed a very Russian balletic style to my gymnastics, which led some people to think I was of Russian descent, though my family tree had German, Czech, and English components. Sometimes they would come up and say hello in Russian. When

I would say hello back in Russian, my accent was a dead giveaway and the person would switch to English.

. . .

Skimming a competition report posted on the German gymnastics news site *Gymmedia* after the Cottbus World Cup, I read the following:

"Canadian newcomer Kyle Shewfelt made finals and, in one of his side passes, performed an artistic full twisting prone dive after a front layout."

"Full twisting prone dive" sounds difficult, but it was, in fact, the easiest skill in my routine. It was just a rebounding straight jump with a full twist, which I landed in a push-up position. A ten-year-old could do it. *I have one of the hardest floor routines in the world and all they remark on is my silly little corner part?* I thought. But people wanted to watch the routine again just to see that move. Everyone in the competition had world-class tumbling. The unique little corner part distinguished my routine from the others. I filed that away to think about later.

In the meantime, I was learning lots about other cultures. "Let's go to the sauna," Sasha suggested casually one day after training.

"Sweet, I love saunas!" I exclaimed. Sasha neglected to mention that in Germany people of both sexes often occupy the same sauna au naturel, so when we walked in I had to quickly avert my eyes. In my knee-length swim trunks, I settled on a wooden bench amidst the steam and the naked bodies, feeling deeply embarrassed. Good thing my skin was so red from the heat that nobody could see me blush.

$$\cdot\ \cdot\ \cdot$$

Gymnastics is not a sport that makes you hate your competitors. Sure, everyone wants to win. But we all understood how hard the skills we did were, and how hard we worked to master them. No matter what flag was sewn on our uniforms, we supported each other and were always glad for those who came out victorious. In gymnastics, the real competition is against yourself.

I became fast friends with Allana Slater from Australia. We were both from Commonwealth countries and bonded over our mutual mastery of sleeping with our feet on the airplane tray tables on long-haul flights. Latvia's Igor Vihrovs was especially nice. Igor was a floor specialist too, and, like me, he came from a country not known for producing great gymnasts. He had already qualified for the Sydney Games and seemed to be building systematically toward the floor final, improving at every competition.

I also developed a strong bond with Jana Komrskova, the Czech women's champion. Jana enjoyed practising English and I loved talking to her. We had tons in common, down to our May 6 birthdays. Jana-chika, as I called her, felt like a long-lost sister and we could chat for hours.

When we weren't training, Sasha, Richard, and I would go sit at nearby cafés, drinking coffee and consuming chocolate-filled pastries. Everywhere we went, we always set aside one afternoon for something unrelated to gymnastics, like going out to lunch in the city centre or seeing a tourist attraction. I loved visiting local grocery stores or corner markets to see the different items they stocked. The cookie aisle was always my favourite. We spent hours hanging out in the hotel playing cards, listening to music, and watching European MTV. Since there was no budget to have a physical therapist travel with our team, we spent a fair amount of time hunting down bags of ice from the hotel bar and taping them to our ankles and each other's shoulders.

Almost every day, I wrote down my thoughts in a journal, trying to find lessons to pull from each experience. Sasha and Rich were generous with their wisdom about competing on the circuit and made it clear that I could always go to them for advice. One of the first things I did in every country was to buy an international calling card and find a phone booth to call my parents and a friend or two in Calgary every couple of days. Homesickness, I found, was a real thing.

In the gyms, I chatted happily with anyone who would speak English. At the post-competition banquets, everyone danced into the early hours of the morning. I started coming out of my shell and even busted out my sweetest dance moves.

Making new friends helped grow my confidence in the gym as well. In Glasgow that April, I won my first world cup medal, a bronze on floor behind Nemov and Bulgaria's Jordan Jovtchev. That's when I really started to believe that the 2000 Games were within my grasp. I even dreamed of reaching the final there, where I would have a chance at an Olympic medal.

But the Canadian Olympic Committee was still not convinced—they wanted a larger sample size. I was at the airport in Glasgow to go back to Canada when I learned that I had been assigned to compete at the Pacific Rim Championships in New Zealand five days later. When we landed in Calgary, I went home, did laundry, slept for four hours, and went back to the airport to catch a flight to Christchurch. It was an intense time of travel and adaptation, but I was completely living my best life and wouldn't have had it any other way.

The next few months were a whirlwind of airports and arenas as we hopped between continents. I was on a roll. In New Zealand, I won gold on vault and bronze on floor. Then we returned to Europe for the final world cup event of the season in Ljubljana, Slovenia. It was June, the Olympics were twelve weeks away, and the competition was becoming fiercer as people began approaching their peak level.

I finished fifth on floor in Slovenia and returned home tired but content. Richard hadn't been able to crack the top eight on his best events and was no longer in the running. I had done everything I could to prove that I deserved that second spot on the Olympic team, but I knew the ultimate decision rested with the Canadian Olympic Committee. All I could do was wait, continue to train, and cross my fingers.

9

THE CALL

THE PHONE CALL CAME ON A HOT AUGUST morning, about a month before the Games.

"Kyle, I'm calling from Gymnastics Canada and I wanted to be the first to congratulate you," said the voice on the other end of the line. "You have officially been named to the Canadian team for the 2000 Olympic Games!"

The moment was extraordinary. I did a joyous lap around the house after I hung up. I kept repeating "I'm going to be an Olympian" to myself.

Kyle Shewfelt, Olympian. It felt so deliciously real.

When I walked into the gym later that day, Kelly was standing on the floor. Without saying a word, I strode up to him, looked up into his eyes, smiled, and threw my arms around him.

"Kelly," I said, "we're going to the Olympics."

I felt light as air that day. I ran a little faster and tumbled with greater ease. I had been like a beast the whole summer, preparing as though I had already been named to the team. When I looked around the gym and saw the kids training beam or running toward the vault, I remembered how I had gazed in awe at Jennifer Wood, knowing she would be an Olympian. Then I applied myself to each of the tasks in the plan, determined to set a good example for all of them.

. . .

My parents always figured I'd end up going to the 2000 Games, but I was superstitious about having them book flights before it was official. They didn't want to put additional pressure on me or jinx anything, so they started planning their trip in secret, though they forgot to hide the incriminating documents. One night, a couple of months before the call came through, I found a printout of possible flight options from Calgary to Sydney on my dad's office desk. The final destination was listed as Sydney, *Nova Scotia*.

I brought the paper upstairs and laid it on the kitchen table. "Um, if you guys are planning on booking flights to Sydney, you might want to make sure they're to Sydney, Australia," I told them, rolling my eyes. "Busted!" Dad chuckled.

They did end up booking a trip to Australia to watch me compete, which was mostly planned under my radar.

"What would you have done if I hadn't qualified?" I asked them later.

"We would have sent you a nice postcard from our Australian vacation," Dad responded dryly.

. . .

I flew to Sydney in early September to join Sasha and his coach, Serge Castonguay. Kelly was not an official coach for the Games, so he was set to arrive a week later. In the meantime, Sasha and I installed ourselves in the Olympic Village.

Since we weren't part of a full team, our living quarters was a portable trailer tucked behind the residence houses where the women's team was staying. Inside were two single beds, twin nightstands, two wardrobes, and a bathroom. It was bare bones, but each of the beds was spread with a bright blue comforter that read "Sydney 2000" with the boomerang-inspired logo of the Games. It may not have been luxe, but we didn't care. We were at the Olympics!

Once settled, we visited the Team Canada admin offices in the Village to get outfitted with Team Canada gear. We left with tracksuits, hoodies, T-shirts, hats, bags, shoes, socks, and an array of other knickknacks and gear. The package also included a podium jersey, a very special article of clothing that we were instructed to wear *only* if we won a medal. There was so much Canadian stuff we looked like we'd robbed a souvenir store.

I had been planning to compete on all six events, so I trained everything during our first sessions in the gym. Problems with the Def flared up almost immediately. I just couldn't get the timing right as I released the bar. After Kelly arrived, we decided that rather than stress myself out, I would compete only floor and vault. I didn't have a real chance at making the all-around final anyway, which was reserved for the thirty-six men with the highest combined scores over the six events. Concentrating on floor and vault, we figured, would allow me to conserve energy and focus on the events where I had the biggest chance of making a splash.

I couldn't get over the image of the Olympic rings. The international symbol of the Games was everywhere in the

Sydney Superdome: on the mats, the equipment, the chalk buckets, the boards behind the chairs off the podium, even the garbage cans. As a kid I often doodled the rings on top of homework assignments, memorizing the order of colours from left to right: blue, yellow, black, green, red. It was surreal to see them everywhere and to be able to trace them with my fingers on the equipment. I let myself be awed for the first couple days and then tried to ignore them, doing my best to downplay the significance of it all. I had a job to do and knew I could lose focus if I got too excited.

Because Canada had only two male gymnasts, only one coach was accredited to be on the floor with the athletes, and Kelly wasn't it. Not that that stopped him from trying. When podium training—our only chance to train in the actual venue on the actual set of equipment that would be used in the competition—began, Kelly got there early and strolled out onto the field of play like he owned the Superdome. That got him in. Unfortunately, he had forgotten to use the bathroom before our session and by the time nature called, officials and volunteers assigned to check accreditations had been posted around each entrance to the competition floor. Kelly held it valiantly for an hour before the urge sent him racing out of the arena. He couldn't come back in and had to coach me from the stands for the rest of the day.

In the meantime, I was struggling with the floor exercise mat, which was from an Australian equipment brand called Acromat. I'd competed on it at the Pacific Rim Championships in New Zealand that spring and found it stiff. In Sydney, it was fresh off the production line and hard as a rock. You had to keep your body super tight and be very fast in your reactions to get any lift out of it, so tumbling passes took much more energy. Everyone complained about how sore it made their shins to punch with extra force, but at least we were all in the same boat. At the end of training, nearly all competitors had bags of ice wrapped around their lower legs.

My goal on vault was to land my two and a half twisting Yurchenko. If I could do it without a major fault, it would be named after me in the men's code of points. But nothing was working that day in podium training. I did the vault over and over and landed on my backside every single time.

Sasha was quiet and tense. In order to maximize his medal potential, he too planned to do only his best two events: high bar and floor exercise. As the world silver medallist on high bar, there was a lot of pressure on him to come home with an Olympic medal.

Training was a little lonely for both of us. Most of our biggest competitors were part of full teams of six gymnasts who moved around in groups and joked with each other between turns. If someone had a bad routine, there was a compatriot or two to pat the gymnast on the back and offer words of reassurance. Sasha and I did not have this luxury. The deck was stacked against us in other ways too: since we would be performing in the very first subdivision, we expected the scores to be lower, because judges tended to leave themselves room to mark higher as the day went on. We would be fighting an uphill battle to get one of the top eight spots for the final on our events, and we knew it.

In order to conserve energy on the night before the competition, we decided not to attend the opening ceremony. The Canadian women's team didn't go either, but we got all dressed up in our special opening ceremony uniforms and watched from the athlete lounge as Team Canada marched into the stadium. Led by veteran Yvonne Tousek, we had our own little parade around the Canadian section of the Village before retiring to bed.

When I was a child, I had wondered what I would think about the night before competing at the Olympic Games. In our tiny trailer in the Village, I lay there visualizing my floor routine over and over, going through all the small details I had worked on over the past several years to put my personal stamp on it.

I once heard an Olympian say the trick to the Games was to pretend that it was just another competition. I considered that for a moment and rejected it. Nope. This was the freaking Olympics, and it felt bigger than anything I'd ever done. Even the butterflies in my stomach were supersized. I had waited twelve years for this day, and in one more sleep I would finally be competing on the Olympic stage.

10

THE OLYMPIAN

YOU COULDN'T HELP BUT LOOK UP—AND THEN up some more—when you walked into the Superdome. The Olympic arena was immense, with a ceiling so high it seemed like it was in the clouds. It was, literally and figuratively, the biggest arena I'd ever competed in, and it was awash in electric blue, my favourite colour. A good omen, I thought.

A decent-sized crowd gathered to watch the first subdivision of men's prelims, even though it was early in the morning and the top teams weren't competing until later in the day. Despite the early hour, there was a freshness in the air, which seemed to vibrate with possibility.

As I stood just off the floor exercise mat waiting for my signal to begin, all my calm completely deserted me and I stood there weak in the knees and quaking with stage fright. *I can't feel my legs*, I thought. The lofty arena, the Olympic rings, and my own expectations all bubbled up at the same time, breaking over my head like a tidal wave. It was a terrible moment, but when the green light finally illuminated on the scoreboard indicating that it was my turn to compete, I raised my arm in a salute. I felt a surge of energy rise up from somewhere deep inside, as though I were a machine that fired up when plugged in. It was go time. I was officially competing in the Olympic Games.

I felt quick and smooth as I flew through my first tumbling pass, a whip back into three complicated twisting elements, each one rebounding into the next. After the final skill in this combination, a front salto with one and a half twists called a Rudi, I let my body soar upward and float back down to the floor to land in a prone position. I was trying to pace myself and make measured movements, but it felt like someone had pressed fast forward and I was getting ahead of myself. I windmilled my arms in the corner, trying to maintain my balance.

Calm down, slow and steady. Breathe.

My second pass, a backwards two and a half twist to a front layout to a front full, was spot on. *Yes!* I cheered in my head, stepping out of it crisply in my best Nemov impression. The third pass didn't go as well: I went in with too much power and landed only a couple of feet from the corner on my full twisting prone dive. There was still a press handstand and rollout to do into the corner, and I didn't have a lot of room. I couldn't afford the 0.1 deduction for going out of bounds if I was going to have a chance at making the final.

I did the press, executed a small pivot and made the roll as compact as possible. I could feel the line judge's eyes boring into my feet, marking the distance from the white line. As I moved toward the corner, our eyes locked for just a second, and then I did a tight little turn, placing my heels directly on the line. As long as nothing went over it, I was safe.

I was almost home free: only the last pass remained, a new double twisting double back flip I had added over the summer. *Deep breath*, the ever-present voice in my head coached. *Strong legs. This is the Olympics, dude. GO FOR IT!*

I ran hard into the final pass and tried to be quick and tight on the back handspring before the takeoff. I got a good upward set and flew through the air, cranking around two flips and two twists in the tucked position. The ground rose up to meet me just as I had hoped it would. I landed on my feet, taking just a small hop forward. I bowed to the judges and felt a big smile spread over my face. I had done it!

I jogged off the floor and looked up into the nosebleed section of the stands where Kelly and my parents were seated. I couldn't see a thing, but I imagined them on their feet, clapping and cheering and grinning broadly. That's when it hit me that I would forever be an Olympian. I could have shouted for joy.

I hop-stepped giddily down the steps of the podium and cast a glance up at the scoreboard. I had been scoring between 9.5–9.7 on the world cup circuit, and something around 9.7 would stand me in good stead for the finals.

Then 9.525 flashed next to my name. Beside it in red was –0.1, meaning I had incurred a penalty, most likely for going out of bounds. "Why did I get a 0.1 penalty?" I asked Serge. I was certain I hadn't stepped out before the last pass. Serge went off to find out. He walked over to the head judges' table and conferred with them for a few minutes.

"You went out on your *first* pass," he told me when he came back. I cocked my head, confused. I hadn't thought I was that close to the line, but when I watched a video of the performance later I saw that when I floated into the prone position after the Rudi a toenail had indeed landed outside the line.

9.525. I sighed. We would have to see if the score would put me in the top eight.

. . .

I rotated around the gym with my group, sitting out pommel horse and rings, half-watching guys from other countries as they hit or missed their routines. Mostly I stayed in my own little bubble, thinking about what I needed to do for vault. I planned to do the Yurchenko with two and a half twists and I needed to focus on that.

The idea that a skill with my name would be done by generations to come was so exciting to think about. Having your own skill meant you had contributed a little piece of history to the sport, setting you apart as a pioneer. It's easy to be like everyone else; the difficult thing is breaking out and doing something nobody has ever done.

But before it could be called my own, I had to land it on my feet. If I fell, I'd have to wait until the next major international competition to try again. As I walked up the steps to the vault podium, I could feel that competitive engine revving inside me again. I stepped onto the blue runway and drew a line at my starting mark with a piece of chalk. Then I drew a big square box, which I coloured in.

Male gymnasts glide down a twenty-five-metre runway on their approach to the vault. My start was at exactly 24.65 metres (86.75 feet), beginning with a small step with my left foot followed by a powerful, gliding step with my right. It may have looked random, but every step in the run had been refined through years of training. The approach has to flow, and if it isn't exact it throws off the entire rhythm of the vault, which can be dangerous for the gymnast.

At the other end of the runway, the green light came on. I saluted the judge and placed my feet squarely in the chalk square. I stared down at the vault in the distance like a soldier staring down the face of a gun barrel, then took the small step with my left foot, followed by the gliding step with my right, and was off like the wind.

I flew down the runway, vaguely aware that there was a mounted television camera matching my distance just beside it. My roundoff was smooth and I got a terrific block off the horse, lifting high into the air with plenty of time to complete the two and a half twists. I landed on my feet and stepped a bit off to the side.

I raised my arms and bowed to the judges, knowing I had done the first-ever Shewfelt in Olympic competition. The score, another 9.525, didn't matter. A century from now, people could still be saying "Hey, nice Shewfelt" to male gymnasts who did the vault well. Having that little piece of history was almost as good as winning a medal.

· · ·

Kelly and I watched the other subdivisions from the nosebleed seats. Kelly laughed as he recalled his experience of watching me compete. "From where I was sitting, you looked like a tumbling ant," he joked.

"As a coach there are some moments that really stick out in your mind," he continued. "For me, seeing you compete out there today and knowing that you achieved your dream of becoming an Olympian is huge. I feel really lucky to have been able to watch you out there. You did a tremendous job."

"I was so nervous!" I exclaimed, chuckling. "There were a couple of times that I just looked around and thought, holy sh--, I'm representing Canada at the Olympics. Could you see my legs shaking before I competed on floor?"

We waited all day to see if I had made the floor final. After the first subdivision, I was in second place. As the hours and subdivisions ticked by, my name slipped down the list, and when everyone had finished, I sat in twelfth place. If I hadn't made that 0.1 mistake on my first pass, I would have scored 9.625, good enough for fourth place and a ticket to the final. A measly tenth of a point cost me the chance to contend for an Olympic medal. I shook my head in disbelief. There is really no room for error at the Olympics when a tenth can make the difference between challenging for a medal and being done after the first day.

In our trailer that night, I wrote a little manifesto about what I wanted to learn and improve. My mind was erupting with new ideas and pouring them out on paper seemed like the only way to capture them. I filled several pages with brainstorms for new combinations and notes about what I needed to do better. I needed to get physically stronger. I needed even more polish on the little details. I needed to earn more credibility on the international scene. I needed more confidence in the moment before saluting the judges. I needed to train like an Olympic champion rather than an Olympian. I needed to take my gymnastics to the next level.

Sasha looked on in disbelief. "You need to relax, man," he laughed. "Come on, let's go to Heineken House and get this party started."

"Maybe I do need to relax," I told him, "but the road to Athens begins right here."

That's what I thought, anyway. But when I met up with Kelly the next day, he was dressed in shorts and sandals, with a sharp pair of sunglasses perched on his head. He did not look like he was in coaching mode.

"So what do we do now? Are we going to train?" I asked eagerly. Kelly looked at me in that kindly way of his, like his most studious pupil had asked for math homework on the first day of summer break.

"No, Kyle, we're not going to train," he said, smiling. "We're on vacation now. You're here for the rest of the Games, and I want you to enjoy it. You've earned it. I'll see you back at Altadore in a few weeks." And with that, he disappeared.

I stood alone on the sidewalk, processing this. Then I began to smile. I was eighteen years old and an Olympian. It was the second day of the Games and I was done. That left nearly two whole weeks to have fun in Australia without having to worry about anything at all. Sasha was right: it was time to party.

11

THE AFTERPARTY

THE FIRST ORDER OF BUSINESS WAS THE TATTOO.

I got my eyebrow pierced in a spur of the moment, I'm-an-adult-now-so-I-can-put-holes-in-my-face decision on my eighteenth birthday, so naturally a tattoo seemed like the next logical step in adulting. A lot of discussion throughout the Village revolves around the symbolic Olympic rings tattoo: where the best places to get it are, how big it should be, the pros and cons of black and white versus colour.

Armed with copies of the Olympic rings cut from the Sydney Morning Herald, Sasha and I headed for Harry's Tattoo Parlour in downtown Sydney, where an artist drew up a rendition from the image and inked it into our skin. Harry's may have been a little scuzzy, but it was open on a Monday, which was good enough for us.

Sasha bravely opted to get his tattoo on his chest. I flinched as the needle dug into the skin on my right shoulder blade, but the result was totally worth it. During the next few days, I went shirtless as much as I could and preened in every mirror I came across, examining my new ink.

In the space of about a week, the main dining hall at the Olympic Village went from being a super serious competition zone to a place of debauchery. Every night the crowd around the Village McDonald's got bigger as more and more athletes finished their events. After months or years of intense training for the Games, the pent-up energy exploded into a wild party scene.

I took advantage of everything Sydney had to offer, including touristy things like going to the Sydney Zoo to meet the koalas with my parents. The Canadian women's gymnastics team adopted me and we spent a magnificent day boogie-boarding on sun-soaked Bondi Beach. British gymnast Lisa Mason and I snuck into the men's 100-metre track-and-field final at the Olympic Stadium, the hottest ticket in town. We hurriedly flashed our accreditations at the volunteer posted at the athlete entrance, covering up our artistic-gymnastics designation with our thumbs and telling her we were pole vaulters. She let us through, and as Maurice Greene from the USA won the gold medal, we were casually perched at the top of the bowl, dead centre on the finish line.

At night, Canadian expats and tourists would congregate at a Canadian-themed bar called the Moose Lodge in Sydney Harbour for beer-drenched parties. At Canada House, athletes and their families and friends could relax and mingle with sponsors and dignitaries amidst maple-leaf inspired decor, while fantastic Canadian musical acts like Blue Rodeo performed on an outdoor stage.

I was there one night when Canadian triathlete Simon Whitfield showed up with his glistening new gold medal, and what sank in about the encounter was how gracious he was with his time. *If I ever win the Olympics, I want to be as approachable as he is*, I thought to myself. Molson Brewing was giving away free beer, Canada was winning medals, and I was eighteen with no sense of my limit. In the early hours of the morning, I shuffled onto a shuttle bus headed back to the Village and promptly fell asleep on one of the bench seats. I woke up to Luce Baillargeon, a female judoka, shaking my leg and saying, "Hey little dude, we're here. Do you need some help finding your room?" Canadians are so nice. I did eventually make it back to the trailer, though I only vaguely remember how. I must have made a pit stop at the Village McD's, because when I woke up ten hours later there were Egg McMuffin wrappers under the sheets with me.

Between nights out, I went to every single gymnastics competition, including trampoline, which was held for the first time at this Olympics, and watched my friends Karen Cockburn and Mathieu Turgeon win historic bronze medals for Canada. In the men's competition, Alexei Nemov was on fire. He was inspiring in Atlanta, but in Sydney he was in his absolute prime. He won gold medals in the all-around and on high bar, a silver on floor and three bronzes, for an even dozen Olympic medals over two editions of the Games.

On floor, I was thrilled to see Igor, my friend from Latvia, win gold. I'd come to admire him so much on the world cup circuit, where he had spent the spring building toward the Games. Sydney was his moment. He, too, had upgraded his final tumbling pass to a double twisting double tuck, but the whole routine was thoroughly precise and that final run was like the cherry on top when he stuck it cold. After the medal ceremony, I caught up with him in the athletes lounge and we exchanged a hug. "Congratulations," I said. We chatted about his experience and then I shyly asked if I could see his medal.

"Of course!" Igor said with a big grin. He took it from around his neck and placed it in my hand. It was much heavier than I had imagined. My emotions must have been written on my face, because Igor looked at me and lifted an eyebrow.

"Maybe it will be you next time, yes?" he said.

Maybe, yes.

As I stood there holding his medal, I remembered that I had placed higher than him at a couple of the world cup meets that season. I had actually beaten the Olympic champion. Me, little ol' Kyle Shewfelt of Calgary, had, in real life, performed in the same competition as someone who had won the Olympics—and placed higher than him!

The realization lit me up. Suddenly, the whole dream I had nursed since I was nine years old—not just going to the Olympics, but winning there—felt within my grasp. As I turned that heavy, shiny new gold medal over in my hands and stared at Nike, the Greek goddess of victory, on the front, I felt a fresh rush of emotion skate up my spine.

In four years, I wanted that moment to be mine.

. . .

A week later, I carefully rolled up my "Sydney 2000" comforter and my unused podium jersey and stuffed both into my suitcase before leaving the trailer for good.

The sun was shining over Calgary as the plane landed. Being home seemed strange at first. Where was all the free stuff? Where were the Olympic rings? But when I walked through the door of Altadore a few days later, there was Kelly in his tracksuit coaching and all the equipment right where it had always been. When he turned and saw me, Kelly's mouth curved into its usual lopsided grin.

"Welcome back, Kyle," he said. "Shall we get to work?"

12

BURNOUT

LIKE SOLDIERS LINING UP BEFORE THE GENERAL, we stood at attention in front of the new Canadian national head coach, Edouard Iarov. Our open faces reflected a mixture of timidity and respect. Edouard stared appraisingly back at us. He rarely smiled.

Edouard, a Kazakh by birth, began his coaching career in the USSR. His greatest pupil was 1988 Olympic gold medallist Valeri Liukin. Years later, in France, he'd moulded a superb junior men's team, several of whom went on to become World and Olympic medallists. In the spring of 2000, Gymnastics Canada hired him with the expectation that he would transform its men's program. Canada had not managed to qualify a full men's team to the Games since 1988. Edouard was there to turn things around.

From the beginning, Edouard made three things clear:

One: he wanted athletes with a high tolerance for pain and stress.

Two: we would push our bodies and minds to the limit in our training.

Three: we would focus on the task at hand, no matter what the circumstances. With that, he put us to work.

Compared to the way we'd trained before, our first few training camps under Edouard were a shock to the system. We practised three times a day, the first session beginning at 7 a.m. The early-morning workout lasted an hour and consisted of nothing but conditioning and strength work. When we finished, our muscles felt like they'd melted. After this, we would eat a proper breakfast, consisting of something hearty like eggs, bacon, toast, yogurt, and fruit. This meal was all you could think about during the last fifteen minutes of the first session, when the granola bar or banana that you'd gobbled up on the way to the training gym had long worn off and it seemed like years since you'd had a proper meal.

If we were lucky, we'd catch a twenty-minute snooze before heading back for round two at 10 a.m. For the next two to three hours we worked skills, combinations, and routines. The final session, held after lunch and a long nap—and boy, did we need a nap by that point—consisted of more conditioning, as well as refining skills and parts of our routines.

After three days and nine training sessions, things started blurring together. We were in the gym, had just been in the gym, or were about to go to the gym. I felt like my whole life had dropped away. Nothing else existed but the gym, conditioning, and routines. It was like the movie *Groundhog Day*, where you woke up every day and did a carbon copy of what you'd done the day before. The pace was intense, and as our bodies started to break down under the strain, so did our minds.

I'd gotten a faint whiff of this kind of training with Eugene and his death conditioning, but Edouard and his training methods were like Eugene times thirty.

How the hell am I going to make it through the next day of training? I'd wonder as I lay in bed at night, too sore to move. The only answer was to show up and see, and somehow, miraculously, we did make it through. Starting was usually the hardest part, but once you got moving and some blood started flowing into your muscles, the soreness dissolved away.

Edouard pushed relentlessly. Kelly began calling him "Fast Eddy," because nothing got past the man. For one of our first training camps, we flew to the British national team base in Lilleshall, England. Five days in, I had done so many reps on high bar that the calluses on my hands tore open and blood gushed out, staining the entire backside of my leather hand grips. As I swung around the bar, every movement felt like vipers were sinking their fangs into my palms.

Toward the end of the camp, our assignment for the day was to show Edouard one routine on each apparatus. I already felt cloudy with physical and mental exhaustion, but knew I had to find a way to push through. It would be highly unlikely to get out of anything with Edouard in charge. Had I been at Altadore with Kelly, we would have pulled the reins back and picked up again the next day. Edouard showed no such mercy. Developing a high pain threshold with him was as important as developing high-level skills. He wanted athletes who could keep their head in the game no matter what the circumstances. Such was his approach to training: you found a way, period.

Edouard stood beside the high bar and fixed me with his intimidating gaze. I shook my head to block out the pain and jumped to the bar. "I'm only going to take one turn," I told Kelly beforehand, "and I'm going to make it through the routine on my first try." It was the only way, because I knew I wouldn't be able to summon the focus to do it a second time.

As Kelly hoisted me up and my hands gripped the metal bar, all I could feel was the weight of my body pulling on the raw skin. The burning sensation was like a scream into the epicentre of my mind, urging me to let go, but I didn't. I wanted so badly to prove to Edouard that I was tough enough to get through it, bleeding hands and all.

I gritted my teeth, blocked out the pain and started swinging. My hands went numb halfway through the routine. When I landed my dismount, I let out an exhaustive sigh of relief, slipped my fingers out of my grips and turned my palms up toward my face. Another layer of skin was gone and the flesh was a bright shade of pink, glistening with an oily sheen. *How many layers can actually rip off before I start seeing my bones?* I wondered. I looked at Edouard, who simply nodded his approval and walked away. I turned and mouthed a few choice words as Kelly mimicked wiping sweat from his brow. It was one of the hardest routines of my life. Every move hurt like hell, but I had done it. Whatever my limits had been before, they had expanded just a little bit.

Our team worked so hard in Lilleshall that we felt a little night out was merited when the camp came to an end. The British guys we trained with were more than happy to give us a tour of the local pubs. As a result, the 5 a.m. call to get the bus to the airport came much sooner than anticipated. Filing past Edouard smelling like a distillery was painful, though not in the same way as doing that high bar routine. Stoic as ever, Edouard didn't bat an eye.

. . .

Being an Olympian didn't change my life on a day-to-day basis. I did become part of an exclusive Olympians alumni crew and got invited to a few events, but in the grand scheme of things my life was relatively unaffected by those three weeks in Sydney. I resumed my high school studies and walked incognito down the hallways of Chinook College, an adult learning facility, where I took twelfth grade math, physics, and social studies. I was just Kyle, like I had always been. I did have a few more articles of clothing with maple leaves on them and the Olympic rings tattooed on my body, but I was still the same guy.

Outwardly, the Olympic glow slowly started to fade. Inwardly, I did feel a little different. Validated, perhaps. At the gym, many of the kids now snuck looks at me out of the corners of their eyes as they practised. Olympians were poised, and not just when the cameras were on them at the Games. I tried my best to remember that, especially when I had bad days and felt grouchy. I couldn't get mad and kick the pommel horse anymore. The responsibility of being an Olympian, I felt, endured long after the Games ended.

Kelly and I went right back to work. My new goals were to do well at the World Cup Final in Glasgow at the end of 2000, and to add some more new skills to my repertoire. With Edouard in charge, I understood that if I wanted to be on future teams, I would need to improve my strength and skill level on every event. Edouard had made it clear that being a one- or two-event specialist was not going to cut ice with him. The goal was to qualify a full team to the 2004 Olympics, so everyone needed to show improvement on every event.

Train, rest, train, rest. The months ticked away. Everything went smoothly for a while. I closed out the year by winning the silver medal on floor at the World Cup Final in December. It was a fulfilling end to one of the best years of my life. As the year 2000 drew to a close, I could feel the momentum propelling me forward.

And then, that spring, it came to a screeching halt.

I'm still not sure what happened. Despite the late-night party-hopping in Sydney, I had come back to Canada in excellent shape and hungry for more success. I jumped right back into the gym champing at the bit. But by the time nationals rolled around in the spring of 2001, I was tired of doing routines and began feeling unmotivated. The clear vision of my future that I had meticulously mapped out in Sydney started to become fuzzy.

There it was: post-Olympic burnout. I had been competing and training full routines for nearly eighteen months without a break, and the Olympic high had worn off. The goal for 2001 was ostensibly the World Championships in Ghent, Belgium, but the thought of a long summer of Edouard camps and doing even more routines filled me with dread, which turned into anxiety. For a while, I just didn't know what to do about it.

The solution occurred to me as I was driving to the gym one day in June. *What if I just didn't go to Worlds?* In an instant, the heavy chains that had seemed to be around my ankles fell away, and I felt liberated. The thought of competing at these Worlds had made me sick to my stomach. I wasn't in the right headspace to endure the next few months and trying to push myself through it struck me as disingenuous, if not dangerous. My gut was telling me to run in the opposite direction.

I sat down with Kelly in his office as soon as I got to the gym. "I don't want to go to Worlds this year," I said, and winced, waiting for his look of disappointment. It didn't come. Kelly considered my statement for a second and nodded his head acceptingly.

"I support your decision," he said. Then he warned me that there would be repercussions. In this situation, Kelly acted in exemplary fashion. He took the punch for me. He went to the meeting with Edouard and the national team coordinator, Karl Balisch, and explained what I wanted to do. He let them be angry and shielded me completely. It would have been a big deal for Kelly to have a world medallist, but never once did he think of his own reputation or pressure me to do something I didn't feel comfortable doing.

It didn't take long for the hammer to fall. My voluntary withdrawal from the world team training squad got me in big trouble with Edouard and Gymnastics Canada. With many of the top Olympic stars now retired or taking time off, the national staff had smelled an opportunity, and to them my refusal to take part in a major competition where a medal or maybe even two seemed up for grabs was outrageous.

I had been personally invited back to Australia to compete at the 2001 Goodwill Games in Brisbane, but in a tersely worded letter, Gymnastics Canada informed me that it had withdrawn me from the competition, though the invitation was not theirs to decline. No 2001 World Championships, no Goodwill Games.

"This decision has affected the morale of the team, will result in a loss of your international reputation and experience, and could potentially affect the overall results of the Canadian Men's

Program," the letter read. "Your progress will be re-evaluated at Elite Canada in December."

I stuck to my guns; 2001 was not my objective. Instead of going to Belgium to compete, I headed for California to clear my head.

. . .

Chris Waller, a 1992 Olympian-turned-assistant-coach at UCLA, took the spray bottle, applied two quick spritzes to his grips, then stepped up to the high bar. He jumped and caught it, lifting his feet to his hands and swinging back and forth into giants.

Chris was one of my boyhood idols and it was a thrill to make his acquaintance at the University of Calgary's 1998 Jurassic Classic Invitational, where he was a special guest. In the summer of 2000, when Chris invited Uldi to be a guest coach at his GymJam Summer Camp in Santa Barbara, I had tagged along. Kelly thought it would be good for me to switch up my surroundings for a week while I prepared for the Sydney Olympics. With their warm and welcoming hospitality, Chris and his wife Cindy had become immediate friends, and when I left they extended an offer to visit them anytime. With my world fraying at the edges in Calgary, I took them up on it.

Finding his momentum easily, Chris wound up, tapped out, and released the bar, cranking two flips and a twist out of his dismount before his feet hit the mat in a stuck landing. He raised his arms and flexed. "Yeah!" he bellowed. "Old man's still got it!" He was thirty-three.

Outside, Los Angeles was baking in the summer heat, but the air-conditioned UCLA Gymnastics Centre was cool and refreshing. Nice as it was, gymnastics and I weren't on great terms. I worked out, but only enough to keep the calluses on my hands from softening and my body limber enough so I could make a quickish return to the gym when I felt the spark again. My friend Colin, a former Canadian national team member who was applying to work on a cruise ship, was there too. We crashed at the Wallers' place in Santa Monica, lazing around the house, drinking beers in the afternoon and soaking up the L.A. scene. Chris and I talked a little about gymnastics and a lot about life, especially life after the Olympic Games.

"Coming down from the excitement of the Olympics is one of the hardest things I've ever experienced," he said. "You spend your whole life dedicated to this goal; you work your butt off to get there and it happens. But then just like that"—he snapped his fingers—"it's done." *You don't climb down softly, you fall off the edge*, I thought.

"It's only natural to eventually come down from that high," Chris continued. "But you've got to trust that with time, and especially some time away, you'll gain perspective and realize the significance of what it means to be an Olympian. You'll find your motivation again. Have faith in that. You've got more to give to gymnastics. This isn't the end, you're just tired. Let yourself relax and recharge a little, man. It's important to listen to your gut."

I nodded. "That's why I came out here," I said.

"Don't lose that," Chris said. "If you know something is right for you—if you *feel* it—then go with it. Don't ignore those feelings because someone else is telling you that you have to abide by their timetable. That's not going to make you successful."

Talks like that were what my tired mind needed.

. . .

I came back to Altadore in mid-August feeling refreshed and wholly certain that my decision to skip Worlds was the right one. Kelly and I attacked a new training plan, one that didn't include any full routines for a couple of months.

By November, I had several key upgrades in the bag. I was especially proud of my new triple back dismount off rings, one of the most eye-catching skills there is. I couldn't wait to show off my new repertoire at Elite Canada, which happened to be in Calgary.

Walking into the Red Gym at the University of Calgary that November was still nerve-wracking. Even though my heart was pounding, I tried to play it cool, going directly over to Edouard and shaking his hand before greeting other coaches and teammates. I was eager to show I had taken charge of my training and made some gains during my self-imposed competition break, and didn't feel entirely comfortable until I stepped up to the apparatus to let the gymnastics do the talking for me. When I saw Edouard after the meet, he was smiling.

"You'll go to the Glasgow World Cup in December," he said, and I suppressed the urge to pump my fist and say *I told you so*. He also forbade me from competing the triple back off of rings ever again. "It makes me feel scary," he said jokingly, pretending to shiver. It was good to know Edouard cared—and that he had a sense of humour.

13

LEARNING LESSONS

I STOOD JUST OFF THE FLOOR, STARING AT THE red stop sign flashing on the scoreboard above the judges' heads, heart pumping a mile a minute. My first World Championships was going just as I had always hoped it would. The goal was two short routines away, and in my head I was already standing atop the podium. I could practically feel that gold medal around my neck. *World champion, world champion, world champion* drummed through my mind.

Two simple routines. *Child's play*, I thought. *I've done so many routines, two more is nothing.* I had not come to Debrecen, Hungary to compete. I had come to win.

The 2002 Worlds were an apparatus-only World Championships. There was no team or all-around competition, just individual events competition: a qualifying round, a semi-final with the top sixteen, and finally a medal round with the top eight from the semi. It was the moment for gymnasts who were really good on one or two events to step into the spotlight.

In other words, a golden opportunity for a guy like me.

On the world cup circuit that spring, I had won all over the place, and headed into the World Championships as the newly crowned Commonwealth Games champion on floor and vault. People expected me to do well. I expected me to do well, too, and I did—so well that I began feeling like the world title was mine for the taking.

I was about to get a big wakeup call.

• • •

For fourteen years, I trained hard, listened to my coaches (for the most part) and tasted success. I thought that was enough. I was mistaken.

In the run up to Worlds, we had a pre-competition training camp in Montreal. We were given a per diem from Gymnastics Canada for our meals, but the only restaurant within walking distance of our hotel in the middle of nowhere was an Italian place with exactly three options for lunch and dinner: extra-cheesy lasagna, extra-meatball-y spaghetti or extra-creamy chicken alfredo. No matter how hard you train, eating rich, high-calorie foods for two weeks straight leads to nothing but a bloated belly.

When we lined up at the end of our first training session in Debrecen, Edouard cast a quick look at my midsection and fired off something to Sasha in Russian, adding a subtle laugh at the end.

"What was he saying about me?" I couldn't help asking Sasha in our hotel room later.

"He said you were looking a little, um, squishy," Sasha replied with a chuckle. "He joked that you look like you gained ten pounds on the flight over here."

Squishy? Ten pounds? I ran my hands over my stomach and tried to flex my abs. I didn't feel heavy, but I'd be lying if I said I felt as defined as I had once been. Although I semi-consciously watched what I ate before big competitions, during the fall of 2002 I had been throwing caution to the wind, and not just in Montreal. I ate what I wanted when I wanted, and you could even see the evidence of my unhealthy food choices on my face. My cheeks were puffy, and patches of acne surrounded my mouth and forehead. Mine was a grilled cheese and french fry childhood, but as a slender kid who could tumble like a tornado, I never worried about my physique. Now it seemed Edouard was doing it for me.

Joking or not, Edouard's observation stuck in my head. In Debrecen, I spent every night in the hotel sauna trying to sweat off a few extra ounces. I took to staring at myself in the mirror and obsessing whether I looked cut enough. I defined myself so much based on my six pack that I began nitpicking myself. *My stomach isn't chiselled*, I thought. *I look like the Pillsbury Doughboy.* I felt extra self-conscious and became very aware of every little thing I put into my mouth. The thing to do, I thought, was to restrict my intake. Eat as little as possible and the extra layer of blubber Edouard had remarked on would become less obvious.

· · ·

Debrecen was Uldi's hometown, and he couldn't wait to show me around. Uldi had moved back to Hungary to try to qualify to the Hungarian team as a rings specialist for these Worlds, but came up short. Bad for him, good for me: I got my own personal tour guide. He even took me to his parents' home for visits and home-cooked meals. His dad talked to me in Hungarian as if I were fluent in the language, which I pretended to understand while Uldi's mom filled my bowl with goulash. I didn't have the heart to say no, even though I was well aware it wouldn't make me look in any better shape. I compromised by taking a few bites, then smiling to indicate that I was full.

Uldi's bedroom was plastered with newspaper articles and medals from his childhood. Nothing in the room testified to the abuse that he'd endured at the hands of his childhood coach; that was a story he would tell later. For the moment, he sat back and enjoyed being home.

. . .

My first routine on floor in the qualification round felt quite effortless. As I did each of my tumbling runs, I remember actually thinking it felt too easy. I qualified to the semi-final in second place, behind Romania's Marian Dragulescu, a phenomenal tumbler and vaulter who was now one of my main rivals.

The gymnastics side of it felt simple. The mental part was much harder. Standing in that corner of the floor waiting to compete during the semi-final, I was so excited—and so completely green.

What goes on in your mind in the moments before you salute the judge is revealing. At the 2002 Worlds, I didn't think about the routine. I figured it would happen easily, just like in prelims. My brain skipped ahead to the happy ending: the podium, the medal, the Canadian national anthem. I focused on the outcome, which I had no control over, rather than the routine itself, which I still had to do.

Staying in the present and not allowing your mind to focus on the end result is a learned skill, just like a backflip—and I was about to learn it.

The first pass was the same series of four rebounding skills that I had performed in Sydney. I got through three of them before I found myself sitting on my butt in the middle of the floor, having misjudged a takeoff on the Rudi.

Oh, sh--. So long, world title.

The error was a technical one. My position coming out of the third skill, a front layout with a full twist, had been all wrong: my arms too low and body too far forward, pinging me down into the mat. Had my "squishy stomach" thrown me off balance? I wondered. Had restricting my diet dulled my instincts?

Or had I been doing it all wrong in my head? I had been so sure I would just be able to sleepwalk through the routine. I hadn't been present enough to understand what I needed to do to correct myself.

I had never fallen at such a big competition, and to come back to myself right at the moment of failure was almost physically painful. I was shocked and humiliated to have made such a large mistake in front of everyone.

Time froze for a second as a dozen thoughts rushed into my head, most of them along the lines of: *Oh f---. Oh f---, you idiot.*

Oh f---, what are you going to do now? I felt my cheeks flush with shame. *There's no point in finishing the routine. I'm not going to win. I'm not even going to make the final.*

Then another, sterner voice took over. *Get up and finish*, it ordered. *Everyone is watching you. Are you going to give up like that?*

I got to my feet reluctantly, knowing I had to save face and be a good sport by finishing. I had learned years ago that part of the honour code of gymnastics—and life—includes making the best of things if you possibly can. It won't always be perfect, but you have to carry on, even if you don't feel like it. In my mind, the whole thing's a blur. I gritted my teeth through every second of it. Of course, after the error the rest was as good as I could do it, which just made me angrier.

I could almost hear the line from the commentator's booth: *If you could just erase that first tumbling pass . . .*

• • •

I stormed down the steps of the floor podium and slumped myself into a chair on the sidelines. *Dumbass*, I berated myself. I felt like standing up and kicking the line of chairs beside me. I felt like throwing a temper tantrum, blaming someone else. Of course, I knew the truth: it was entirely my fault. It was my fault for being too relaxed and assuming it would be easy. For having the potential to win and letting the chance slip through my fingers.

As soon as he could, Uldi took me outside for some fresh air. By this time, anger was fast turning to embarrassment. *My big chance and I blew it*, I thought.

Uldi grabbed my shoulders with both hands and looked directly into my eyes. "What were you thinking about before the routine?" he asked.

That seemed like an obvious question. "I was thinking about winning the World Championships!" I exclaimed.

Uldi was reflective for a while. Finally he said, "You know, Kyle, the result comes *after* you do a great routine. If you're so focused on winning, you'll be so busy thinking about it that you won't be able to concentrate on what you have to do before you can celebrate. You were living in the future. During competition, you have to live in the present."

My World Championships didn't end with that floor routine; I still had to compete in the semi-final on vault. Floor was my best chance to medal, but I did have the potential to make the vault final. "What's done is done," Uldi said. "You can't go back and try again on floor, but you can go and nail two awesome vaults. It's your choice."

I went back inside and nailed my vaults. There were no podium fantasies before them, but no medal either. I made the final and finished fourth. It would be a year before I got another chance—and at that point, something even bigger would be on the line.

. . .

Kelly wasn't in Hungary because he couldn't take time away from coaching the other boys in his bustling program, but I told him about Edouard's comment as soon as I got back because it was still weighing heavily on my mind.

Kelly leaned back in his chair. "I'm going to be brutally honest here," he said. "I've definitely seen you in better shape." I gulped, but he had already thought of a simple solution. "Why don't we set something up with a sports nutritionist through the Canadian Sport Centre Calgary?"

That's how the excellent Kelly Anne Erdman came into my life. Kelly Anne, an Olympic cyclist herself, had me do a body composition test, and the results showed that I had 15 percent body fat. Together, we set a goal of getting it down to 7 percent. Kelly Anne asked me to record everything I ate for five days, and then did a complete evaluation of my diet and suggested some areas where I could make better choices. She recommended that I eat something high in protein within thirty minutes of the end of each training session to help rebuild muscle. She suggested that having three smaller, more balanced meals and three nutrient-rich snacks per day would help curb most of my unhealthy cravings.

Apples dipped in peanut butter became my favourite go-to. Proteins needed to be a part of every meal and the portion size as big as the palm of my hand, while fresh fruits and vegetables should take up the largest majority of my plate, she counselled. Carbs were definitely on the menu, but they needed to be whole grain rather than the refined whiter versions. When I proudly told her that I often drank juice rather than cola, she countered that it still had a lot of sugar and water was better than anything. Finally, she advised that I limit my rich and high-calorie food intake to special occasions only. The key was enjoying these in moderation.

My family got on board as well. Brown rice and whole-wheat bread and. pasta became staples in the pantry. Instead of cooking with red meat, we took to preparing grilled chicken and ground-turkey-based dishes. The fridge got stocked with pre-cut fruits and vegetables for easy snacking. No longer did I eat jumbo chocolate chip muffins for breakfast. Two poached eggs with a lower-fat cheese on a whole-wheat English muffin became my new morning sustenance. Everything I ate became about fuelling my body rather than quenching my appetite. In this way, I became a more holistic athlete. I had always believed that training in the gym was good enough. Now I began to understand that everything you do outside the gym has an effect on your performance as well.

Gradually, from 65 kg (143 lbs) I leaned out to 62 kg (137 lbs), what I came to consider as my ideal competition physique. I felt light and confident when I looked in the mirror, yet still strong on the equipment. By the summer of 2003, I was in the best shape of my life. Good thing too, because our team's biggest challenge yet was right in front of us.

14

CALIFORNIA DREAMIN'

IN ANAHEIM, OUR TEAM, COACHES, AND SUPPORT staff filed into the hotel room for the war council. It was early evening, and outside the sun was setting on a soft, glorious California night. People plunked down on chairs, sat on desks, and stood against the wall as we arranged ourselves into a circle. I sat on the floral comforter on one of the queen beds, humming with energy.

I was confident. No, more than confident. Invincible. I was in peak form and couldn't wait to compete. *Here I am, world. Just try and stop me.*

When your mind and body meet in preparation, the feeling of readiness that wells up inside you is one of the best things in the world. Only a few times in my career did I feel that rare sense of absolute mastery over my performances. The 2003 Worlds was one of those times.

The last weeks were always intense and difficult, but on the eve of the 2004 Olympic qualifier, I was more fired up than I ever had been heading into a competition. *Enough training,* I thought. *I'm ready to get out there and show what I've got.* When you just can't wait to go out and pounce on the equipment, that's when you know you're ready. And I was ready. You could have gotten me out of bed at 3 a.m. with a bullhorn and I would have been able to hit my routines cold.

Good thing, too. The next day's competition would define a lifetime of work for my teammates and me. The top twelve teams would qualify to send a six-person squad to the Athens Olympics, and we wanted more than anything to be among them. There would be one of two outcomes: jubilation or heartbreak.

• • •

During the past four years, behind every hard training camp, every routine with ripped hands and every tumbling pass with sore shins, the goal of getting back to the Olympic Games as a team was on our minds. The seven of us who trained together to prepare for the Olympic team qualifier in Anaheim—Sasha, Richard, Grant Golding, David Kikuchi, Ken Ikeda, Casey Sandy, and me—were determined that 2003 would be our year.

By then Sasha had won so many world cup titles on high bar that he could use them as paper weights. Richard was a peaceful warrior, whose way of working through frustration was to deepen his focus. Grant was a workhorse—nobody did as many repetitions as he did. Dave was Mr. Consistency. Ken, Richard's little brother, could bring in big scores on pommel horse, the team's weakest apparatus. With the way he improved every day, non-competing team alternate Casey pushed us at every practice to be better than we thought we could be.

Then there was me: springy, zingy, and fuelled with warrior assurance.

Once we were all comfortably installed, Edouard began going over the final lineup and strategy for the team competition the next day. After several minutes, he fell silent. I lifted my head. A moment had come.

"I just want to say: I guarantee I'm going to hit every single one of my routines tomorrow," I said forcefully, looking around into every guy's face as I slashed the air with my pointer finger. "I'm going to own every skill, stick every dismount. We want to go to the Olympics. We're going to get this done."

If life were a sports movie, another guy would have stood up and said, "I'm going to hit all my routines and stick all of my dismounts too, dammit," and then the other guys would have echoed that. By the end of the scene, we'd all be standing in a circle yelling and pumping our fists, electrified to go out and be our very best. Aaaaand scene.

In reality, my proclamation was met with an awkward silence. Finally Dave shyly half-raised his hand. "Um, I'm not willing to go as far as *guaranteeing* that I'm going to hit all of my routines," he said, smiling, "but I do feel pretty good."

Okay, it wasn't the rousing motivational scene you see in the movies, but the fact remained: we were one team, with one goal. We wanted to go to the Olympics *together*. And the next day, we were going to leave it all out on the floor.

• • •

In the 1960s, a psychology professor named Bruce Wayne Tuckman developed a theory that came to be known as

"Tuckman's stages of group development." His theory went that groups striving for a common goal undergo several developmental stages, including "forming" (the first time the group comes together), "storming" (in which the group gels, individual members are assessed, and any disagreements are resolved) and "norming" (where a spirit of cooperation emerges). "Performing," the final stage, is one in which the team has a shared vision and is willing to do anything necessary to accomplish its goal.

We had competed against each other since we were children. We had nodded at each other from across regional gymnasiums as adolescents and travelled the world as young men in the developmental and junior systems. We had fought to prove our superiority, our merit for spots on the world team. We had been through the forming, storming, and norming stages. We understood each other's quirks. We all knew our specific roles. We accepted and celebrated differences in personality, training style and needs.

Now it was time to show what we could do.

• • •

We started on parallel bars. As the weakest link on this event, I was dropped from the lineup. Dave went first to set the tone. As I paced back and forth on the sidelines, every guy hit his routine—a solid beginning.

High bar was next, and that's where I saw action for the first time. I had one job to do on high bar: get a good score to set up Sasha, the anchor on the event. After nailing the best high bar routine of my career, chalk dust erupted into the air of the Anaheim Pond as I gave Sasha a high-five at the chalk bucket.

Floor was next, and I breezed through the routine. I even stuck my dismount, a rarity for me, as I usually took one small hop backwards for security. *That should get me into finals,* I thought as I cheerfully zipped off the floor.

We got through pommel horse and rings, our two weakest events, and headed to vault to close out the day. Once again, I was the anchor. I squinted down the runway, staring at the table in the distance.

I'm going to hit every single one of my routines tomorrow. I was alone, but I knew that I was not the only one doing this vault. Five men were standing with me at the end of that runway. Five sets of feet sprinted with me. My teammates were lifting me up.

I hurdled into my roundoff, hit the springboard, flew backwards, and pushed off the table, up into the two and a half twists of the Shewfelt vault. And when I came down, I planted my feet on the mat and didn't move an inch.

Booya!

I didn't try to stick that landing. It was just there and it felt like magic. I still had to do a second vault to qualify for the event final, but for the team, the first score was the one that counted.

As I walked back down the runway to take my mark, I saw my teammates and coaches at the end of the runway, jumping up and down and losing their minds. I smiled a bit as I turned my focus back to the vault. I felt light and powerful as I flew down the runway a second time and lifted into the air. When my feet hit the mat, I finally allowed myself to celebrate a little, too. I galloped off the podium and got practically dogpiled by my teammates. As we locked into a group huddle, arms linked tightly around each other's shoulders, we jumped around letting out hoots and hollers full of boyhood joy. We knew that this had been exactly the day we had imagined as we pushed ourselves through all of those challenging training sessions. We delivered on our expectations. And we had done it together.

• • •

After that, everyone settled down to wait.

Canada had competed midway through the qualification rounds, and we wouldn't know where we stood until every team had finished competing. We bit our nails through the rest of the subdivisions, watching from the stands as the teams we considered our closest rivals—Germany, Italy, and Spain—moved around the gym.

As the day wore on, we fixed our attention on Belarus. In 2001, the Belarusians were world team champions, but in the years since they hadn't produced similar results. Once again, in Anaheim they had a very rough day. When we saw their final team score below ours, we knew we had it. Canada finished ninth, well inside the top twelve.

Much later that night, we stood on the balcony of a hotel room, beers in hand, and clinked bottles to celebrate what our hard work and intense preparation had brought. Disneyland stretched in front of us, and that night there were fireworks in the park. We watched them rise into the sky and explode with colour and light and felt bound forever by what we had accomplished. It was a warm August night, thirty degrees Celsius and humid, but it felt like Christmas.

Canada was going back to the Olympic Games as a team.

. . .

I lay back in my lounge chair by the pool and surveyed the scene before me with satisfaction. To my left, the guys from one of the Scandinavian teams were doing flips into the pool. Members of several others were splashing around in the shallow end, laughing and having fun. It was gymnastics spring break. *Worlds should be held in California every year*, I thought.

I was at the pool on coach's orders. "Kyle, your requirement for this week is to do a good training in the morning," Kelly said. "In the afternoon, your co-assignment is to go hang out by the pool and get some vitamin D." Kelly knew me well enough to know that in the days between the team qualification and men's floor final I would sit in my room and stress over every little movement if he didn't make me go out and take my mind off things. He was right—instead of losing my focus, this mental time off made me stronger.

A few days later, I was back on the field of play for floor finals, with vault the day after. Once again, the careful preparation paid off, and I hit a strong, dynamic routine. The little artistic touches Kelly and I had put in caught people's attention. *International Gymnast Magazine*, the magazine I tore through as a kid, profiled me in an article called "The Style of Kyle." *Inside Gymnastics Magazine* named me as one of their "50 Most Photogenic." Seeing my name in those magazines always lifted me up, and being recognized for my style made me feel even more special.

The floor final was stacked with talented contenders. Everywhere you looked was someone who did beautiful, amazing gymnastics. There was the newly minted all-around champion, Paul Hamm of the United States; Olympic medallist Jordan Jovtchev from Bulgaria; world silver medallist Diego Hypolito from Brazil; my old friend Igor; and Marian, the reigning world champion on floor.

Plunged into a field this deep, I wasn't sure what to expect. I ranked first after the qualification but I knew that we would be starting from zero and it was anyone's title to win. A year earlier, I'd entered the semi-final focused on the end result, thinking, *I'm going to be a world champion.* This time I modified my pep talk.

I'm a good gymnast, I told myself over and over as I stood at the edge of the floor. *I've found my place in the sport. I belong here, and I'm going to show everyone why.* The green light came on and I raised my right arm in a salute. The moment had come.

During the next seventy seconds, I could feel the audience lingering on every element and holding their breath as I flowed through my routine. In finals, only one apparatus is contested at a time, so all eyes are on you. You can feel the collective attention of the arena following your movement. Every cough, every child squirming in their seat, every ooh and every ahh—you hear them and sense them. Sometimes you can even hear the judges' pencils scratching on their paper, scribbling away. And though you're hypersensitized to it all, you're so fully immersed in the task at hand the distractions are white noise.

Everything came together in that exercise. The only thing more I could have asked for was not to have had quite so much power on my dismount. As I landed it, I took a small slide backwards, the only noticeable mistake in the routine. I prowled around on the sidelines as the last competitors performed. When the final scoreboard flashed and I saw my name in bronze medal position, I jumped up and hugged Kelly. My first world medal! Cross that one off the dream list.

I won bronze with a score of 9.737, while Jordan and Paul were crowned world co-champions, each with a score of 9.762. I was elated, but later, in the back of my mind, I couldn't stop reliving the hop on the dismount which cost me 0.1. Had I stuck it, I would have been world champion.

Along with the bronze I won on vault a day later, I left Anaheim feeling fulfilled. Coming so close to gold provided an incredible sense of motivation.

Athens, I thought, *I'm coming for you.*

15

PATIENCE

"DO YOU THINK YOU CAN WIN THE OLYMPICS?"

The question caught me off guard. Once again, I was in front of a TV camera. But I wasn't nine anymore and the Olympics weren't a pipe dream.

In the spring of 2004, *Sports Illustrated* published its big Olympic preview edition, including a rundown of the twenty-eight Olympic sports and carefully researched predictions of who would medal. In men's gymnastics, they had pegged me to win gold on floor. Seeing my name with a little gold-medal icon next to it in the biggest sports magazine in the world gave me a jolt at first, but I was warming up to being considered a gold-medal contender.

I took a breath and looked the journalist in the eye. "Yeah," I said. "Yeah, I think I could."

I spent the week after Worlds hanging out with friends in L.A., then returned home to train for the big year ahead. As the calendars flipped to 2004, all of a sudden there were many visitors in the gym. Journalists were calling asking if they could bring camera crews to film training and do interviews as the Olympic press machine hummed into motion.

It was a special time for Kelly as well. At the end of January, during our first national team training camp of the year, he and his girlfriend Sue, who was also a coach, came up while I was stretching at the end of a training session.

"Kyle, we have something important to tell you," Kelly said. I looked up at him, concerned. "Important" things are always life-altering things, but then Kelly and Sue exchanged a smile. "We're pregnant!" they exclaimed.

"Well, I'm pregnant," Sue clarified.

I jumped up and hugged them. "That's great, you guys! Congratulations!" I said. Then a thought occurred to me. Sue didn't look pregnant. "Wait, when are you due?"

Sue's smile faded a little bit. "That's the thing," she said. "We aren't far along at all, but we knew it was important to tell you right away. I'm due at the end of August."

"During the Olympics?" I felt a big lump form in my throat. Kelly had a hell of a sense of timing.

"Hang on," Kelly said. "We've talked it over, and I want you to know that no matter what, I will be with you every day you compete in Athens, through floor and vault finals. I promise you that. We have come this far together, and seeing this dream through with you to the end is my number one priority. I am not going to abandon you during the last lap of the race."

"If I have to have this baby without Kelly by my side, I will," Sue added. I was touched by their devotion. I knew how much I would need my coach in Athens. That he was potentially willing to sacrifice seeing the birth of his first child was a testament to the strength of our bond.

My goal for the 2004 season was simple: I was going to go out and dominate every meet on floor. I wanted the world to know that I was the clear and definitive Olympic favourite. I would deliver my best routines at each and every world cup and glide into Athens prepared for anything.

Then in March we went to Cottbus World Cup, and everything went sideways.

· · ·

The dots connected at the beginning. My floor routine put me in first place heading into finals and I headed to vault feeling great. I got through my first vault with ease. On the second, a Kasamatsu full (a roundoff onto the vaulting table with a *double* twist off), I was a little low as I pushed off the table into the twist. I was still getting into competition shape, so the vault lacked some amplitude, but I'd done the skill so many thousands of times that I had a complete sense of where I was in the air.

Of the two, the Kas was clearly the easier vault. It was supposed to coast me through qualifications and into finals, where I would add an extra half twist. But as I pushed off the table, a little warning light flashed on in my mind. The landing would be low, I sensed, though instinctively I knew I wasn't so low that I would have to put my hands down and spoil the vault.

I did make it to my feet, but my left ankle crunched as it hit the mat. I made a move to the side, only to discover that I couldn't really lift my left foot. *Hmmmmm. I couldn't have broken my ankle*, I thought. That would have really hurt. At the same time, suddenly I couldn't put any weight on it.

To save face I kind of hopped my feet together, putting weight only on the big toe of my left foot, and saluted the judges, then limped off the mat like a dog with a frozen paw. Kelly swooped in within two seconds and sat me down. "What's the matter?"

"I don't know," I said honestly. My face was red with panic. "I crunched my ankle coming down. It's a sharp, deep pain."

"Take a second and then try to walk it off," he suggested. I stood up and hobbled around a little, but my nerve endings shrieked indignantly whenever my foot came in contact with the floor. I had thought I could deal with pain. Over the course of the past few years, I had bashed my Adam's apple into the high bar, taken a knee to the eye socket in the foam pit, and sustained several dislocated fingers and sprained ligaments. But here was pain I had never felt before and couldn't deal with.

A German trainer looked at my ankle and said it was probably sprained. Kelly and I agreed on the only course of action available: ice and Advil. I crossed my fingers and hoped I would wake up for finals the next day and find it had all miraculously healed overnight.

• • •

I lay in bed the next morning and cautiously moved around. *Maybe*, I told myself, *when I look at my ankle everything will be normal.* I sat up and slowly pulled back the covers, exposing my leg to the sunlight streaming into the room.

My ankle was the size of a grapefruit and a deep purply yellow, like an eggplant. Everything was definitely not normal.

"Yeah, you're not competing today," Kelly said when he saw it.

I sighed. So much for world domination.

• • •

I flew back to Calgary with crutches and had an MRI a day later. It showed a talus-bone contusion: a bruise of the biggest bone in the ankle. The sports physician announced that it could take six months to heal, and I felt my stomach sink to my feet. The Olympics were in August, five months away.

There is nothing you can do about this, I told myself. *The only thing you can do is to go to physical therapy, visualize your routines, and keep yourself strong so that when it does get better you can train the way you need to before Athens.* My daily routine, which had previously revolved around two training sessions, now expanded to include appointments all over the city: the physical therapist, the chiropractor, and massage therapist, all before or between practices.

It was frustrating, because I was young and strong and hungry and impatient. In the gym, I did everything I could aside from tumbling and vaulting, but before long I felt like this injury business had gone on long enough. I figured the weakness was in my mind, not my body, and there was only one way to snap myself out of it. I stepped onto the power tumbling track, a long, bouncy stretch of floor used for learning new skills, and decided to do something simple: three back handsprings into a takeoff, pushing off the mat with my legs and rebounding into the air.

The force of punching out of the third back handspring, driving my feet down into the floor in order to get the push up into the air, nearly destroyed me. It felt like a sledgehammer had smashed into the inside of my ankle. I collapsed onto a mat at the end of the track and lay there like I was dead. The pain lingered like a stubbed toe and all I could do to ease it was hold my ankle in the air and not move it.

Kelly came over, looked at me sprawled on the mat in agony, and sat down.

"You're not doing yourself any favours, you know," he said gravely. "You think you can just push through this, but that's not how this works. Your bone is bruised on the inside. Imagine what would happen if you had a bruise on your arm and someone came along and punched it. The bruise would get worse, right? That's how this is. You're going to end up setting yourself back even further if you make impatient decisions, so smarten up. Now, how about some ice on that ankle?"

I could only groan my consent.

• • •

The media requests kept coming. We did our best to oblige every journalist who wanted to do an interview or a story. I was psyched that gymnastics, largely ignored by the media in non-Olympic years, was finally getting some attention, and felt proud to promote the sport.

But after several rounds of questions about going to the Olympics, performing at the Olympics, and what it would be like to win Canada's first medal in artistic gymnastics at the Olympics, the external pressure started to overwhelm me. The Olympics were four months away and I couldn't tumble. My ankle wouldn't be 100 percent until well after the Games. Talking about making the Olympic team when I wasn't even sure if I would be healthy enough to go made me feel like a fraud.

The uncertainties tumbling through my head at all hours of the day began affecting me at night. Unable to shut my mind down, I started having trouble sleeping. I decided to enlist Hap for help. He had remained a constant sounding board ever since my rebellious teenage years, and I was hopeful he could help me navigate through this new challenge.

Sitting in the same big green leather chair I had been in for nearly a decade, I stared through the cracks in the drawn blinds into the parking lot and spoke my biggest fear aloud. "What if I'm not good enough?" I asked.

Hap attacked the concept from a different angle. "Maybe, just maybe, you've done this to yourself," he said. "Remember Sydney, when you didn't even know you had qualified until just a month before the Games?" I thought back to the time when things seemed less complicated and there were fewer people to disappoint, and sighed.

"Well, you weren't ranked third in the world then. You hadn't just won a plethora of world cups. You hadn't earned your reputation just yet. So what if you look at it this way: you've earned these expectations. This is *your* doing! If you were ranked fiftieth in the world, nobody would be expecting a medal. The goal would be just to get to the Olympics again. But you aren't ranked fiftieth. You're ranked third. You are one of the best. You have earned this expectation." Classic Hap, always turning lemons into lemonade.

"Also," he continued, "you've got no control over what others think of you and what their expectations are." At this point he stood up, pulled a fountain pen from his shirt pocket and started waving it around in the air as if he were conducting an orchestra. "You've got no control over the judges. You've got no control over your competitors. You've got no control over the spectators, the equipment, the venue, the buses, or the weather on competition day," he said, emphasizing the last word of each sentence with a strong flick of the pen. "You have zero control over the outcome. You could be at your best and someone else could be better. The only thing you have control over here is your performance." The pen was now pointed straight toward the space between my eyeballs. "When you are in that floor final, the only thing you will have control over is yourself."

It was a very *Way of the Peaceful Warrior*/Socrates moment and the perspective shift was like a lightning bolt that jarred me right out of my skin.

"Kyle, it can no longer be about the external victory, the gold medal. I know that becoming an Olympic champion has been your dream since you can remember, but now that you're this close, you need to shift your focus.

"What will your best routine look like? Imagine a performance you are proud of where the result doesn't factor in. What will you say to yourself before you step onto the floor? What will your execution look like during your tumbling passes? What will the rhythm of the skills feel like as you rebound across the floor? What will your internal dialogue sound like as you compete? And how, in the next few months, do you want to remember your preparation? Do you want it to be stressful, where you are wasting energy worrying about what others expect of you, or do you want to enjoy it?

"Because if you are focused on the outcome, let me tell you right now, you are in trouble. But if you can focus on the subtleties of each and every moment in the routine, you might stand a chance at making it to the top."

With that, Hap took the fountain pen and scratched something across a prescription pad. I felt hope rising within. A mild sleeping pill would be just the thing. Then Hap handed me the sheet. It read:

B.R.E.A.T.H.E. Each letter was bold and distinct.

"Breathe," Hap repeated matter-of-factly.

I looked at him. "I would have preferred a sleeping pill," I said.

"Use this prescription when you're feeling overwhelmed," he instructed. "Take ten big deep breaths as many times a day as required. Don't worry, breathing has been cleared by anti-doping. And you can't overdose."

When I got into the car after our meeting, I sat holding the steering wheel and paused for a moment. I took a few deep breaths, in through my nose and out through my mouth. As I did, I repeated to myself, *I can only control my performance. I can only control my performance . . .*

• • •

The Olympic Games didn't scare Kelly, or if they did, he was really great at hiding it. He made sure our workouts were efficient, and that I followed the plan. My only jobs were to show up motivated, do my numbers, polish my skills and protect my ankle. As the days got longer, I was finally able to start to put things together again in the gym. It no longer hurt to punch into takeoffs. I was vaulting into the foam pit. The conditioning to keep the rest of my body in shape was paying off, too: I wasn't too far from my pre-injury form. I became a pro at taping my ankle and I had been given a prescription for a strong anti-inflammatory medication that was working wonders.

One Saturday in mid-June, we took a day off for a special event at a yacht club in Burlington, Ontario, as Kelly and Sue got married.

I was his best man, and we wore matching black suits and sweated bullets on the hot, humid Ontario day. Sue, her pregnant belly sheathed in a cream-coloured dress, was radiant and uncomfortable. During the reception, I made a small speech and thanked both of them for their unwavering support. Kelly, I told him, was not just my coach, he was family. And I deeply appreciated the sacrifice he and his new wife were making for me.

As we danced the night away, visions of Athens kept popping into my mind. These visions were always present, even when immersed in life's monumental moments. When you dream about something your whole life and then it's right in front of your face, it's all-consuming. When all you have to do is reach for it, that's when things can get overwhelming.

The talus-bone injury brought me back down to earth and made me realize how fragile the Olympic dream was. Nothing was guaranteed, no matter what *Sports Illustrated* predicted. Still, the injury turned out to be a blessing in disguise, because it put my focus on healing and just getting back to the Games. It became an important distraction as I prepared for the biggest performance of my life. I finally understood that the outcome, whatever it was, would be the bonus.

16

ATHENS

AT THE CALGARY AIRPORT, KELLY HANDED ME an envelope. "DO NOT open until we land in Athens" was written on the front. I carried it in my bag on the flight from Calgary to Madrid, where we had our pre-Olympic training camp, and then from Madrid to Athens. As the plane's wheels touched down at Athens International Airport, I tore it open.

It read:

Kyle,

I wanted to share some thoughts with you as you embark on this final phase of your journey.

1. You are a winner already. You've done 16 years of training and competing and you're getting the chance that you have dreamed of all your life.
2. You are not defined as a person by your result at the 2004 Olympics. You have already defined yourself as a person. You are a great person and gymnast!

3. The people in your life love and support you through good times and bad.

4. You can rely on your great experiences to help you through the pressure moments that you will experience when you compete.

5. Your focus has been amazing through all of the camps.

6. Just hitting your routines will put you in a great position for the finals.

7. Staying positive will help you enjoy one of the greatest moments of your life.

8. Family, coaches, and friends will support you to the end.

9. Your coach is very proud of you!

10. Your gymnastics looks wonderful and very classy. You are a head above the rest. "Public eye can pick that one out."

11. Don't forget to enjoy each moment. Time will pass and you will look back on it one day.

12. Be a good sportsman.

Your coach,
Kelly

A big grin spread across my face as I considered fate's role in my journey. How lucky was I that my mom chose Altadore that day sixteen years ago. Without Kelly's patience, protection, and long-term plan, I never would have made it to the Olympics. Eugene could be proud—he'd developed into a pretty great coach.

. . .

Athens was simmering with Olympic excitement. That special atmosphere unique to the Games attached to us from the moment the plane landed. There's something magical about arriving in the Olympic host city. Seeing those five coloured rings plastered on every wall, every sign, even every garbage bin never gets old.

The Olympic Village is like the coolest summer camp you can imagine. After we picked up our accreditations and checked into our three-bedroom apartment, we ran around like little kids who had just passed through the gates of an amusement park. Everywhere I looked, I saw rainbows and pots of gold.

We peeked into the internet café, with its rows upon rows of computers. We checked out the main dining hall, and its huge cafeteria with specialties from around the globe seemed even bigger than it had been in Sydney. I decided that I would eat exactly one cheeseburger and one small order of french fries on that first day, which would curb the temptation until I was done competing. Boring salads and grilled chicken would be the go-to menu for the next two weeks, but I wasn't about to completely deny myself my beloved french fries. Moderation, Kelly Anne had said. It's all about moderation.

One of the first things we received was a special gold coin from Coca-Cola. Inserting it into any of the drink machines dotted everywhere around the Village got you as many free drinks as you wanted.

Outfitted with our new Team Canada gear, we quickly fell into the pre-Games routine. There was no nonsense in my Olympic training, especially after we arrived in Athens. I had my twice daily training plans written out and followed them to the letter. I didn't take extra turns. I didn't mess around. Every movement I made was calculated. "Get in, get your work done, and get the f--- out," Kelly said. I got in, got my work done, and got the f--- out.

There was so much confidence-building power and momentum in that efficiency. No distractions. Total presence and focus on the task at hand. The best part was that it felt fun.

During one of our first training sessions, I ripped off a Shewfelt vault right out of the box, without even doing a warm-up timer, and stuck the sucker cold. If I had been in a video game, bombs would have exploded all around me as my feet hit the mat. As I walked back to the end of the runway for another, my chin was held high, my shoulders were back, and positive self-talk was coursing through my mind.

I was there to win. That's right: I was there to win. I wasn't cocky—I was laser focused. I knew my timing, and the way my body and mind should feel.

Despite some lingering pain in my ankle, I was in peak condition. Kelly kept my confidence high by continually reminding me how great he thought I looked. He knew all I needed at this point was positive reinforcement. The numbers had been done during the past several years. I had earned my reputation and learned how to compete under pressure. Now was about tapering off, confirming my readiness with each turn, and waiting.

When you're ready, waiting is just torture. During the first week in Athens, I tried to live in a slow, meditative world, and walk a slow, meditative walk. I was quiet and focused nearly twenty-four hours a day. There would be moments when the adrenalin would start to bubble up and I'd have to push it down. No, I told myself, it's not time to get excited just yet.

. . .

The main dining hall was a good ten- to fifteen-minute walk each way from our living quarters, and when you're used to walking only a few steps through the parking lot from your vehicle into the gym, these additional steps start to take their toll on your muscles and joints. After two days, I began to feel my shins getting sore from walking a mile on concrete three times a day, so we switched to a smaller dining hall that was closer to our residence. We were "conserving energy," as Dave put it.

In the bubble of the Olympic Village, the internet café became my lifeline to the outside world. I sent an Olympic update email to my friends and family every couple of days. I missed everyone terribly and would call them occasionally from the new Canadian-flag-themed flip phone I received in my swag package, generously donated to each Canadian athlete from Bell Canada. We were warned that we would receive a bill for anything over 100 long-distance minutes, so I kept my conversations short. The upside of the Village, besides all the free stuff, was that being in such an energizing yet secluded place lifted most of the distractions and left me with plenty of time to spend in my head.

At the Olympics, you can be surrounded by people and still be in your own little world, often visualizing your ideal Olympic performance over and over and over again. One day, I passed my friend Perdita Felicien, the reigning world champion in the sixty-metre hurdles, outside one of the Team Canada buildings.

"Hey," I said, trying to grab her attention, but she ignored me and stared at the ground. Years later when I reminded her of the moment, she apologized and explained that she was just in her zone and hadn't noticed me. I totally got it.

There were distractions if you wanted them. There was a games room, a "discotheque," a movie theatre, and a fitness centre and swimming pool, but I didn't spend a lot of time outside the room Sasha and I shared. Like Perdita, I began spending a lot of time being Zen, taking deep breaths, not talking much, and furiously writing in my journal.

Thinking that you've prepared for this event for so many years and here you are and it's almost go time isn't comfortable, especially at first. When I was a kid, I would feel sick to my stomach before big competitions, worrying about all the possible scenarios that could unfold. At the Olympics, when I felt myself getting overwhelmed and jumping out of my skin, I would put pen to paper.

"The winners are the ones who can get comfortable being uncomfortable," I wrote, "because no matter what people are trying to project on the outside, we are all terrified on the inside. We're all as invested. We've all dreamt this same dream a thousand times over. This is THE MOST important moment in all of our lives to this point. So, the battle will not be on the competition floor, it will be who can get the most comfortable in all of this discomfort beforehand." Writing down my thoughts and feelings became my way of escaping the Olympic excitement that was always just outside the door. I used the pages to sort out my problems and to make action plans to conquer any possible hiccups that may arise. I wrote out the most obsessive-compulsive lists, including a "competition day packing list," because I was petrified of forgetting something important like my competition uniform or accreditation. I didn't want my anxious squirrel brain to make an appearance on competition day and leave me out of sorts . . . or without my shorts. After a few days, I felt totally settled and confident that I had prepared for every possible scenario. But on Friday, August 13, the night before the qualification competition began, my body went completely rogue.

• • •

This is not at all the way I pictured the Olympics beginning, I thought as I clutched my stomach in agony.

Like in Sydney, there was no chance of us walking in the opening ceremony, because men's prelims began the next morning. There, we would try to earn a place among the top eight nations and qualify to the team final. I also had my eyes set on floor and vault finals, taking me one step closer to an Olympic medal.

Since we weren't attending the opening ceremony, Sasha, Grant, Dave, Ken, rookie Adam Wong, and I got into our Team Canada gear and met in the Village gathering area. You could see a sea of red and white from our Santorini-esque white balcony. We posed for photos, and then the athletes marching in the opening funnelled into line and departed. "Have fun!" we called. We went back inside to watch them on TV in the athletes' lounge.

I remember so little of what we saw that when I watched it months later it was like seeing it for the first time. My eyes looked at the TV screen, but all I could see was myself doing my floor routine over and over.

After the Canadian contingent marched in, I went back to our room and immersed myself in my pre-competition ritual. I gave my hair a fresh buzz, very much like that movie where a Navy SEAL recruit takes a pair of scissors, cuts out chunks of hair, and then buzzes it clean. You can see the steely, transformative shift in their eyes as they go into warrior mode. Shaving my hair down had become a pre-competition ritual. It made me feel sleek, powerful, and centred. I wanted no distractions. I didn't want to waste any headspace on finding the perfect side part I had obsessed about as a kid. Then I went to bed.

I had been laying under the covers for twenty minutes when it hit me. My eyes were closed and I was focused on my breathing when a hurricane of nerves overwhelmed my senses. I tried to fight it off as a wall of panic mounted throughout my body. My stomach began to hurt, badly. I kicked off the covers, ran to the bathroom, and was gut-emptyingly sick. When I emerged an hour later, there was nothing left in my body.

Much later, I learned the anti-inflammatory medication I had been taking for my ankle injury should always be ingested on a full stomach. I hadn't paid attention to those instructions, often taking it first thing in the morning without food, and it had eaten away a part of my stomach lining. So my late-night bathroom party was mostly, though not completely, about nerves.

Eventually I realized that whatever was happening was not going to resolve itself, so I dialed the team doctor and embarrassedly explained my situation. He was understanding and asked me to come to the small medical clinic set up by the Canadian medical team. When I got there, he handed me a foil package with two white pills, assuring me that they would not cause a positive drug test.

"You may not poop for a week," he said, "but it will cure you."

"I'll be happy if I never poop again," I told him.

When I finally got back to bed, it was after 2 a.m. I lay awake and stared into the darkness, wondering how things had gone so off the rails. *This was not part of the plan*, I thought as I slowly drifted away into a light sleep.

Eventually the sky lightened and the day we had anticipated for so many years was upon us. It was a relief to get up and be moving, even though my stomach still felt awful. "Are you okay?" Kelly asked me at breakfast as I deeply exhaled with each attempt at swallowing some yogurt and muesli.

"Kelly, I've been sick," I said miserably. I told him about the stomach cramps, the doctor, and his magic pills. Kelly's face darkened in concern.

"Well, Edouard will think your abs are extra defined today then, won't he?" he joked. "I feel for ya, bud. Not in the plan, but try not to let it rent too much space in your head. You're ready. Please be positive and not let last night's detour define your mindset for today. Try to eat something—you'll need the energy. Just think: you only have to do four routines today!"

I spent the majority of the Olympic warm-up curled in a ball on a mat doing nothing at all. The stomach cramps were almost unbearable. Finally, with forty-five minutes left before we marched into the arena, Kelly came over and nudged me.

"Kyle, you have to get going," he said gently. "This is the Olympic qualification. You have to do a little bit of warming up, okay?" On one of the most important days of my gymnastics life, I jogged lethargically around the floor and went through the motions of stretching. I did some basic tumbling, but none of my big passes. I ran down the vault runway and executed a simple layout Yurchenko and a timer for my second vault. I swung around the high bar and did some simple elements. I didn't attempt the Def. On rings, I put on my grips and did one turn of swings and a handstand. From the outside I probably looked like I was about to implode, but by that point it was about conserving energy in order to have something left for the competition.

When the warm-up was over, we gathered our gym bags and lined up behind the redheaded volunteer with glasses holding a KANADA sign. A few minutes later, to the sounds of music and announcements inside the arena, she began to move forward. We filed behind her, out of the semi-darkness of waiting and into the bright lights of the Olympic Indoor Hall.

17

QUALIFICATION

THAT'S WHEN THE SWITCH FLIPPED.

It was like electricity amped through every cell in my body. With each step toward the arena I felt myself getting stronger. In the three minutes it took to walk from the warm-up gym to the competition hall, my state of being completely transformed. I went from nothing to Super Kyle.

As we came through the entry, there was a loud roar from the crowd. I immediately caught a glimpse of my family in the stands, wearing maple-leaf-shaped hats and waving Canadian flags. *They've got those dorky hats on again*, I thought momentarily. My cheering section included my mom and dad; my Auntie Janice; my girlfriend Melissa, who was a coach at Altadore, and her mom Debbie; and a handful of friends who had travelled from Canada to support us. My aunt and Melissa held up a sign that read: "KYLE SHEWFELT: COULDN'T BE CUTER," to attract the attention of Canadian host broadcaster CBC.

My family flew into Athens the evening before qualification began, made the trek to their hotel via taxi and ferry, slept for about five minutes, and got up at 6 a.m. to get the early boat and make sure they'd be there to see us. "We took wet-wipe showers," Mom informed me later.

Seeing everyone there cheering us on had the same effect as ingesting a home-cooked meal. My stomach cramps evaporated and I was able to put my competition blinders on.

Things were smooth and solid from the start. We began on vault. I went up last. I stood at the end of the runway and took a short, deep breath. Here we go, I thought, and jetted off toward the springboard.

On my first vault, the Shewfelt, I exploded off the table, wrapped into the two and a half clean twists and lightly floated into the landing. I nearly stuck it and knew it was tidy in the air. The judges wouldn't be able to take much in the way of deductions. As I bowed, I felt my face break into an Olympic-sized grin. My second vault, the Kasamatsu with one and a half twists, went equally well. It was one of the cleanest I had performed in competition, the only imperfection a small hop to the side at the end. I allowed myself a small fist pump as I walked off, jubilant. *Yes!* I thought.

The team moved to parallel bars next. Just as in Anaheim, I sat this event out. Instead, I strapped my grips on for high bar and put my jacket over my shoulders to keep warm while my teammates performed. As I watched them compete, I kept myself busy by visualizing the routines to come. I did my best to listen to the positive voice inside my head as the small waves of doubt tried to crash over my mind.

Despite one small flicker of hesitation on a handstand, I did my job on high bar. The Def was floaty and extended as I caught it. After that, we moved to floor—the big one for me. It was the place I knew I could make the biggest statement at these Olympics, but first I needed to make it through the qualification round cleanly.

I was so relaxed during the routine that it kind of felt like a training run. *This is odd*, I actually thought as my body mechanically went through the motions of the exercise I knew so well, *I don't actually feel like I'm competing in the Olympics.* I seemed to be hovering somewhere over my own body, watching myself with great interest as I performed. In Sydney, I could barely feel my legs before I competed. I got overwhelmed by the Olympic weight of the moment, rushed things and made a mistake. Here it was as if I were walking on air.

Only the dismount, that difficult double double, brought me back down to earth as I took a small slide backwards on the landing. Of course I wanted to stick it. Anaheim had proven how a small hop could make the difference between gold and bronze, but because of my ankle injury, I hadn't been able to absorb the extra force of a stuck landing in training. I didn't want to risk further injury by taking a short landing and potentially crunching my ankles. The plan was to take a small hop in qualification to protect my ankle. We knew that if I hit everything else in the routine, I would likely make the floor final. By taking the hop, I knew I would get a deduction, but I also knew I was going to fight with everything in my body to stick it in the medal round.

As I walked off the floor, my teammates all gave me high-tens. When the 9.737 score came up, I was very confident I had made the Olympic final and felt both relieved and energized.

As the lowest potential scorer on pommels, I sat this event out too, and it went by in a blur. With floor out of the way, I began to enjoy myself. Before rings, I sidled slyly up to Edouard. "You don't need me for this event, do you?" I joked. "Can I just be lifted to the rings and then immediately drop off and stick my landing and bow to the judge? I'll be awarded a perfect zero."

Edouard turned his serious face toward me. "We need your score for security," he responded. "Make sure to show them your best iron cross. And no triple backs!" he added with a wink. The routine took thirty-five seconds and passed faster than any rings routine I had ever performed in my life. My double twisting double tuck dismount complete, I saluted the judges and felt myself relax, just a little bit, for the first time in many weeks.

It was a happy, happy day. After our subdivision, I went out into the Athenian sunshine to meet my family in front of the venue. I hugged them all for the first time in more than a month.

Our team goal had been to break into the top eight and get to the team final, but it wasn't to be. With a few mistakes, we came in eleventh overall. I qualified to finals on floor, as expected, behind Gervasio Deferr of Spain and Marian. On vault, making the final was the goal, and I qualified fifth, higher than I'd expected. I knew that my best chance to win an Olympic medal was on floor, and I knew I needed to begin re-gathering my mental strength for the final, scheduled for 8:00 p.m. on Sunday, August 22. There was just over a week to wait.

First, however, I had an entire day off. My family and I met in the Plaka, the main hub of the Olympic city, with its clusters of restaurants and bars. We sat out on a rooftop patio at Canada Olympic House overlooking the Acropolis, which was lit up in the background. The whole setting was sublime.

I was sipping a beer—my first in months and the only one I'd have before the final—and feeling enormously content, when my phone rang. It was Nathalie Cook, the Canadian gymnastics team's media attaché. A producer from CBC had invited me to be on the primetime show that evening for an interview with Brian Williams, the legendary host of Canadian Olympic coverage.

I got wide-eyed. "Brian freakin' Williams wants me on his show?" I laughed. "Of course I'll go, but only on one condition: I need my family to join me. We're in the Plaka at Canada Olympic House."

"We can do that," Nat said eagerly. Six minutes later, an official-looking white van rolled into the Plaka and all six of us piled in. As we zigged and zagged through the streets of Athens to the International Broadcast Centre, it felt like we were in a scene from a Greek car-chase movie.

We got to tour the CBC studios before I sat down with Brian for a five-minute segment. He even called my family on set and had them join in on the interview. I couldn't stop smiling. Doing that interview with him was as much an Olympic *wow* moment as competing itself.

. . .

At 7 a.m., the door opened and Sasha staggered in, looking a little worse for wear.

"Hey," he said, kicking off his shoes and flopping face down on his bed.

"Canada Olympic House?" I asked.

"Heineken House," he replied, his face muffled by the pillow.

There is an unspoken rule in the Olympic Village: you can't be loud and party within the confines of the security gates. In Sydney, I learned that the only acceptable place for late-night shenanigans is the main dining hall. There is also a no-alcohol rule, though some teams figured out how to smuggle beer into the Village. Athletes who don't compete until the last day deserve the same peace and quiet as those who compete on the first. That said, the energy begins to shift as days go by. As more events finish, the dining hall becomes littered with super drunk people eating cheeseburgers for breakfast after coming home from the epic parties. As someone who still has to compete, it gets harder than ever to stay in your own little world.

So Sasha and I made a pact. Since I still had to train and he didn't, he lived it up at the Olympic parties for me every night with the ever-growing number of athletes whose events were done. And since I had to sleep at night and he didn't, we made a deal that if the party was rockin', he wouldn't come back before the sun was up.

Adam, the youngest member of the team, quietly decided that he was going to accompany me to every training. He was eager and wanted to keep in shape, and was also highly motivated by his first taste of the Games and wanted to absorb as much of the Olympic energy as possible. His enthusiasm reminded me so much of myself after I was done competing in Sydney. Every morning when I came down to breakfast, Adam joined me and we went off to the gym together afterward. "See you tomorrow?" he said after every session. "Yup, see you tomorrow," I replied.

Kelly, Adam, and I trained alone. Edouard left after the team competition, though not before meeting with us and asking if it would be all right for him to go home. He was ready to be back with his family and he had faith that Kelly and I could execute our mission.

"If you need me, I will stay," he assured us. Kelly and I looked at each other. "I think we've got this," I said, "but thank you." So Edouard went home to his family, and watched the rest of the Games from his living room in Ottawa.

. . .

After the high of qualifications, I came down a little bit. Things just felt a little off and I struggled to land my tumbling passes well in training.

"Why don't I feel as good as I did before?" I asked Kelly in a panic.

"Don't worry," he assured me. "You're good. You've got this. Let yourself come down a bit, and then let's build back up for Sunday. It's a waiting game. Just keep doing your numbers, keep yourself in shape, and you'll start feeling better." Kelly himself never looked anxious about anything. His job at that point was to keep me from losing my cool.

Our entire team went together to watch each night of gymnastics as it unfolded. In men's team finals, a superb Japanese team carried off the gold after a tight battle with the Americans. The Romanian women never gave an inch en route to a formidable team victory, and Carly Patterson, a talented sixteen-year-old from Texas, stood her ground to win the women's all-around over Svetlana Khorkina.

But it was the men's all-around that got everybody talking. Halfway through the competition, Paul Hamm, the 2003 world champion, had cruised into the lead. Then, on vault, normally one of his best events, he made a small miscalculation that turned into a big error. He landed his Kasamatsu one and a half with his centre of gravity low and way off to the side. In trying to fix the mistake, he careened off the mat and landed on his bottom, right in front of the judges' table.

We thought there was no way he could win with a fall. Paul must have thought that too, but his next two events were two of the strongest routines I'd ever seen anyone do. Those flawless performances, combined with mistakes from almost everyone else challenging for the podium, cleared the way for Paul to regain first place. He joyfully stood atop the podium as the American anthem bellowed through the arena, the first U.S. all-around gold medallist in the history of men's gymnastics, ahead of South Koreans Kim Dae-eun and Yang Tae-young.

Paul's jubilation would be short-lived. Almost as soon as the medal ceremony was over, the South Korean delegation filed an official protest. Yang's score on parallel bars was incorrect, they said: he had done a routine valued out of 10.0, but the judges had credited him only 9.9. Had the judges gotten it right, Yang's score would have been a tenth higher and he, not Paul, would have won the gold. The rules allow delegations to file a score inquiry if they think their gymnast had been unfairly scored, but they have to be quick about it. It wasn't until after the medal ceremony that the Koreans realized anything was wrong. Now they were crying foul.

The affair quickly gained traction in the international press. The improbability of Paul winning the gold medal despite his fall and nagging questions about errors by the judges fanned the flames of the scandal. Many people, including some from Paul's own federation, suggested that he return the gold medal, as though that would make the judges' mistake right. The instant it was suggested, Paul was put in a terrible position. If he gave it back, it would be terribly unfair to himself. If he didn't, he'd look like a huge jerk. It was the judges' fault, yet the athlete was taking the blame.

I didn't let myself think much about what had happened until I read that Paul was being pressured to give his gold medal back. "They should give them both a gold medal," Adam opined the next day. *That seemed fair,* I thought. Paul had had his moment, but I still felt angry for him that anyone had the audacity to suggest that he ought to give it back.

Of course he shouldn't do that, I thought. *Not after the ceremony has happened and he's been declared the winner before the whole world.* And then another idea popped into my head: *How could the judges have gotten it so wrong?*

The Paul Hamm/Yang Tae-young controversy was the first indication that something was going on with the scoring in Athens. Unfortunately, it wouldn't be the last.

• • •

On the morning of my first Olympic final, I rolled out of bed in a relaxed and chipper mood. When I looked at myself in the bathroom mirror, the face gazing back at me was serene. This wasn't normal on a competition day, but it was a pleasant surprise for those who would be spending the day by my side. I'd been weird, grumpy, and easily irritated on meet days since I was a kid, and people had learned that I had a tendency to snap if they tried to get into my bubble.

The morning workout went quickly and easily. I was smiling and taking photos on the floor with Kelly and our team physiotherapist, Diana Perez, who had become a trusted confidant and friend. I was cracking jokes, focused but happy.

Kelly, well accustomed to my competition-day moods, asked if I was all right. Leading up to the Games, he had been trying to instill the idea that I had mastered the sport. "You've put in the hours, learned how to compete, seen what works for you and what doesn't," he said many times. "Now you've mastered it." That final morning training went so smoothly; what he had been saying had finally sunk in.

That morning there was an article in the press about how no Canadian had won a gold medal at the Games, even though eight full days of competition had already been contested. I had intentionally limited my media consumption, but this is one of the few things that filtered through. Just for a moment, I allowed myself to fantasize about ending the drought.

I thought about all of the great Canadian artistic gymnasts who had come before me and paved the way. A handful had even made an Olympic final. The last to do so was Curtis Hibbert, who qualified to three at the Seoul Games in 1988, the year I started gymnastics. I couldn't help but wonder if I would be the one to finally break through.

In some way, I had been preparing for this moment since I was six years old. Sixteen years of preparation for a routine that was going to last seventy seconds. It was August 22, 2004. It was the Olympics and I, Kyle Shewfelt, had the chance to win Canada's first-ever artistic gymnastics medal in Olympic history—and the first Canadian gold of the Games.

18

MAKE IT HAPPEN

NO MATTER WHAT I DID THAT AFTERNOON, I couldn't stick my first tumbling pass. I wasn't even physically doing it. It was all happening inside my mind, and I still couldn't get it right.

I can't stress the importance of visualization enough. Being able to lay back and mentally put yourself in the state you'll be in when you do a routine can be as valuable as physical practice on the equipment. A small percentage of gymnastics is physical. The majority is in your head.

As I lay in my bed on that hot Athenian afternoon before the floor final, I was deeply immersed in the mental imagery of what was to come. With eyes closed and arms relaxed at my sides, I imagined myself stepping into the vastness of the arena, breathing in the humid chalky air, and feeling the tickle of the light blue floor carpet beneath my feet.

I tried to visualize my first pass. I would do my first run and mess it up. I couldn't stop imagining the landing without a step or a hop. I would reset and try again—and mess it up again.

I began to panic. How was I going to be able to stick the routine in the competition if I couldn't even do the first pass right in my head? My breath started coming in raggedy gasps. I was aware of each second that ticked by, bringing me closer to the moment the final would begin.

I was on the verge of freaking out when I remembered a Mark Tewksbury interview I came across after the Barcelona Games. In it, he talked about how he tried to nap in the afternoon before his Olympic 100-metre backstroke final. Butterflies circled in his stomach. He wondered if he was capable of winning the most important race of his life. But instead of thinking that everyone was going to crush him, he thought, *You know what? There are eight guys in this final. One of us has to win. I've worked hard. I'm prepared. Why not me?*

Why couldn't it be him? He went on to win an Olympic title that day.

And why couldn't it be me?

In different corners of the Olympic Village, everyone in my final was probably lying on their beds at this exact moment trying to visualize their perfect routine. *Maybe*, I thought, *the winner will not be the one who is the most perfect, but the one who is most adaptable.* What if I visualized myself adapting to every possible scenario and making small adjustments as needed?

This turned out to be an incredibly helpful perspective and allowed me to refocus. When I finally pictured a routine I was confident with, I felt reassured. Good thing, too, because by then it was time to eat, shower, and head to the arena. As the white door to the room clicked shut, I couldn't help but wonder if the next time I opened this door it would be as an Olympic medallist.

I was quiet as the bus made its way toward the arena. I took the window seat and Kelly sat beside me, making sure to shield me from any potential distractions. As the lone Canadian in the competition on this day, I did our team warm-up solo. When I look back at candid shots taken by Diana during the warm-up, my expression was the perfect combination of intense focus, wide-eyed wonder, and, yes, the look of a person scared silly.

After a general warm-up, I moved to the floor for basic tumbling, a progressive sequence of acrobatic and handstand elements starting with the most fundamental one in the book: forward rolls. I had been doing this exact same sequence at almost every training session and competition for the past ten years and felt blanketed by the familiarity. Finally, I did my first full pass.

My competition-day plan included sticking my first tumbling pass once in the warm-up, and I was determined to have one under my belt before the competition began. I made five attempts, taking a small step or hop on the landing of each one. I was visibly frustrated by the time Kelly waved me over.

"I know you really want to, but you don't have to stick one now," he said in his calm, ever-so-Kelly way. "You just have to do it in the meet. Trust yourself that you can nail it when it really counts. You always do." That was all he said, and it was all I needed to hear.

When the doors opened to spectators thirty minutes before the competition began, we moved back into the warm-up gym. Tony, who was there as one of our team coaches, commandeered the little stereo by the floor and popped in Tom Petty's *Greatest Hits*, one of my favourite albums. As "I Won't Back Down" and

"Runnin' Down a Dream" played in sequence, I felt a small sense of serendipity budding inside me. I kept my white Team Canada tracksuit on as I paced and tumbled around the floor, waiting for the official go-ahead that I was on deck.

We could wait in the warm-up gym as long as we wanted, but we had to be in the competition venue and ready to go by the time the gymnast ahead of us began his routine. I was fifth up, preceded by two of my toughest rivals, Jordan and Marian.

As we walked through the back hallway toward the competition venue, I kept my eyes glued to the ground. I didn't want to watch anybody else compete and I didn't want to see or hear the scores. Sounds were present but ambient, as though I were underwater. I could feel the adrenalin pumping through my body and all I could do to keep calm was focus on inhaling and exhaling.

You've done the work. You are ready, I kept reminding myself. I could feel Kelly's presence just a few steps behind me. As I stood staring at the arena entrance doors, I took one last breath, then nodded. It was time.

The doors opened and the first thing I saw directly in front of me was Marian standing in the corner of the floor, waiting to begin. Over the loudspeakers, I heard the announcer say, "The score for Jordan Jovtchev of Bulgaria is a 9.775." So much for knowing nothing.

I kept my back to the floor as we walked in and set our bags down. From the cheers that erupted around the arena as Marian finished, I knew he had done well. I continued to look at the ground, but held my hand out to him in a brief gesture of congratulations as he walked down the steps of the podium past me, heading to the waiting area off the floor.

Kelly accompanied me to the edge of the podium. A few feet from the steps leading up to the floor, he laid his hand on my shoulder, just as he had the day we met. I looked up and we made eye contact.

"Kyle, I just want you to know that no matter what happens here today, you have my love and support. You look great and you've worked so hard," he said. "No matter what happens, we're all so proud of you. Now go out there, show it off, and enjoy this."

Looking back, I wonder how long he agonized about what to say in that moment. Had he been preparing those words for the past sixteen years? It was a wonderful speech, and if I hadn't been so in my zone I would have hugged him or at least smiled. As it was, I didn't really react. I just nodded slowly in gratitude, inhaled deeply, and closed my eyes. I certainly felt moved by his belief in me.

Then Kelly stepped aside and I climbed the steps to the podium.

．．．

And the internal conversation began.

You've got this.

I held my head high, but kept my eyes down.

Don't make eye contact with any of the judges. They can detect nerves.

Deep breaths.

You are so prepared.

Good rhythm. Smooth whip back. Be ready. Get your arms up on the takeoffs. Fight.

I walked around to the corner of the floor. My mouth felt pasty. My heart was thumping so loudly in my chest that I could hear it pounding in my ears. I tried to look calm. I secured the beige tape around my ankle, adjusted my gymnastics shoes and shook out my arms. Marian's score would be coming up soon.

As I waited for the signal before I could salute the judges, seconds felt like hours.

Marian's score appeared. I was talking to myself and didn't hear it. I kept repeating positive mantras.

You are here. Be present. This is your opportunity. Good rhythm. See the floor. Fight for your landings. Show off the corner parts.

Then, out of the corner of my eye, I saw the green light.

Go time.

I took one last deep breath, in through my nose and slowly out through my mouth. Sixteen years of work for a seventy-second routine. This routine.

Let's do this.

I raised my arm and stared right through the judges. Even though they were right there, I didn't see them.

I pointed my toe and took a step onto the floor, heel hugging the white line. As I did, I said the words out loud: "Make it happen."

It was my motto of these Olympic Games, something I had practised during all the training sessions leading up. It was about creating comfort, and this phrase settled me into the right state of mind.

Make. It. Happen.

I set the other foot carefully in the corner of the floor and stood still for a split second. Then I went on autopilot, letting

the years of physical and mental preparation do the work
and succumbed to the end result. I was fully immersed in the
moment. My mind was crystal-clear and, for a moment, not a
single thought fluttered in.

I raised my arms, slicing them in front of my body and
up above my head, my chin lifting slightly. Then I turned my
hands outward and slowly lowered them down so they ended
up straight out to the side. I paused for a heartbeat, then swung
them back and then forward in a crescendo, making sure to keep
them straight as boards, and hurdled into my first tumbling pass.

Kelly had been right: I completely nailed it. On the outside I
looked calm and cool, but on the inside I was doing a celebration
dance. My second pass was a little off because I vaguely heard
someone in the audience yell "Go Kyle!" right before I entered
into the two and a half twist, but I adapted and executed
smoothly. Only an expert could tell that I made a quick balance
adjustment with my arm and had a flicker of foot separation, but
I knew it and my heart jumped into my throat.

One by one, I executed each of my skills. I could have done
each of these elements in my sleep. With every movement, the
ever-present narrator in my head issued tiny reminders.

*Point your toes. Knees straight. Float it. Hold it there. That
was good. Take a breath. Halfway done.*

I was in the zone. The audience applauded as I settled into
the splits after my trademark full twisting prone dive.

Lift your chin. Lifting your chin is like the period at the end
of a sentence. It's one of those little things that adds style and
shows confidence. *Canada's never won an Olympic medal in
gymnastics. You've got to stand out when you're from Canada.*

The press to handstand is a simple skill, but a staple of nearly every men's floor routine. Gymnasts are required to hold it for only two seconds, and they were the longest two seconds of my life. I had been doing handstands for as long as I could remember, but never in the Olympic final as the world watched. Time seemed to slow down.

Extend tall through your shoulders. Grip the floor with your fingers. One one thousand. Two one thousand.

The routine had been as good as I could have hoped to this point. All I had left was the dismount—the most important dismount I would ever do.

I took one last big breath and prepared for my final tumbling pass. Sticking the landing would decide the fate of the routine. *Run a little slower than normal so you'll be in total control on the landing.*

I ran three steps, my heart thumping out of my chest and my eyes glued to the corner of floor that would be my landing zone. The chatter inside my head took on a more intense, urgent tone. *Stick this dismount, Kyle. Stick it. STICK IT.* And somehow, I knew I would. I had never felt so sure of anything in my life.

Not too much energy, I told myself. *Slooooow.* I stepped forward and I felt like I was running in slow motion. I took off, soaring ten feet into the air. Two flips. Two twists. As I cranked into the second flip I saw the floor below. My vision narrowed into it. It seemed to rise to meet me as my legs stretched toward it, and the instant they touched, they melded into one.

My toes sunk into the ground. Then my heels. I landed like an arrow in the bullseye of a target and didn't move a muscle. My hands were clenched, the veins in my neck bulging. My face was definitely purple. I wasn't letting this one go.

And I didn't.

I stuck that landing, and as I did, an incredible rush of elation coursed through my entire being. That landing was the culmination of sixteen years of my life. All of that work came out in that one moment, in the routine I'd always dreamed about. I'd been preparing for it since I was a child. That dance between me and the mat decided everything.

I had known for months this was coming and I had been amassing the energy of every cell in my body for that landing. It took everything I had. I was tired for a year and a half afterward.

I put my head down for a second and brought my hands together. Then I threw my arms in the air, clapping my hands and pumping my fists. I didn't know what I was doing, I was just reacting. It was completely uninhibited and every movement came from a place of total joy.

Then I was running off the floor, down the steps of the podium and into a big bear hug from Kelly. When I think of the Olympics, that's what comes to mind—that hug after that routine. We didn't know the score or if I would have a medal. All we knew was that I had done my absolute best. There was nothing more I could have given, nothing more I could have done. Experiencing a moment like this, when you know you've reached your ultimate potential, is one of the greatest feelings in the world.

When the score—9.787—came up, I was in gold-medal position. Though Marian had also received a 9.787, tiebreaking rules were in place. Later I found out that five of the six judges' scores were equal and had cancelled one another out, but one did not. I had received a 9.75 to Marian's 9.7, and that made all the difference. There were still three gymnasts left to perform though, so I wasn't home free. *Okay*, I thought. *If my score is better than just one of theirs, I'll have an Olympic medal.* Gervasio, the next up, didn't better my score.

Bronze, I thought. Then: *Hey, if my score beats the next guy's, I'll have silver.* And then it did.

Last to step onto the floor was Paul Hamm. His routine was typical Paul, just stellar. But on the landing of his final pass, he windmilled his arms and took a step. That wouldn't be enough, I knew. He wouldn't catch me. It was over, and nobody had surpassed my score. Marian would have silver, Jordan bronze.

A solitary thought whirled through my mind, over and over again:

I'm an Olympic champion.

Holy sh--.

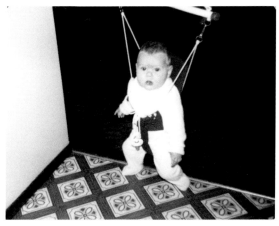

Even as a baby,
I loved jumping

With Mom, Dad and
Scott when I was
three years old

At six years old
when I started
gymnastics,
I loved the
foam pit

Showing off my splits in the living room at age seven

I quickly realized that hockey wasn't the sport for me

With my idol, Jennifer Wood, in 1992. I was so in awe that I could barely look at her during this photo shoot

At eleven, I was a little perfectionist-right down to my slicked hair and toe point

Competing on parallel bars at the 1996 Canadian
Championships with Kelly looking on

My first national team uniform warranted an
awkward hallway photo taken by my mom

Murray Trimble

Kelly offering post-routine advice when I was fifteen

Alexander Jeltkov (Sasha) and me having a break during Sydney 2000 podium training

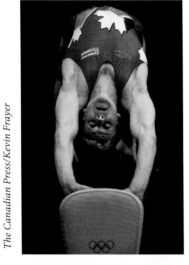

Performing the first Shewfelt vault during Sydney 2000 qualification

I had the time of my life in Sydney - here I am having a laugh with my pal Yvonne Tousek

Grace Chiu / Graceclick, 2002

Competing the Def on high bar at the 2002 Worlds

Diana Perez

Standing on my first Worlds podium after winning
bronze on floor exercise in Anaheim 2003

Our entire team was feeling happy after the qualification competition in Athens. From left – Tak Kikuchi, Adam Wong (back), Grant Golding, David Kikuchi, Ken Ikeda, me, Tony Smith, Sasha

Diana Perez

My family and me with Brian Williams at the CBC studios in Athens. From left – Mom, Debbie (Melissa's mom), Brian, Auntie Jan, Melissa, Dad and me

Feeling uncharacteristically relaxed after morning training on the day of the Olympic final - with Diana Perez and Kelly

Diana Perez

Diana Perez

I was getting very frustrated during the warm-up, but Kelly reminded me to trust that I always deliver when the pressure is on

Diana Perez

Soaring high on my dismount during warm-up -
Kelly was always keeping me safe

I have never fought as hard as I did on my
dismount landing during the Olympic final

Kelly and I share a very special moment
after learning we had won gold

With Dad and Mom on the concourse level of the Olympic Indoor Hall. Without their support and love, I would have never achieved my dream!

With Chris and Cindy Waller at an epic Athens afterparty

Returning home after Athens was a whirlwind of excitement

Doing a post-Olympic press tour with fellow Canadian Olympic medallists Adam Van Koeverden (left), Simon Whitfield (middle) and Alex Despatie (right)

With Uldi on the set of *White Palms* in Budapest

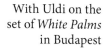

Our 2006 World Championships team where we placed sixth. Back row from left – Edouard Iarov, Adam, me, Tony (back), Brandon O'Neill, Ed Louie, Ken; front row – David and Nathan Gafuik

Moments after breaking my legs in Stuttgart as they scan my knees for ligament damage – I was in complete shock

I was in rough shape after having surgery back in Calgary

At a press conference with Dr. Nick Mohtadi as we explain the extent of the injury to the media

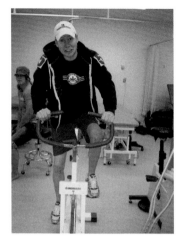

I spent countless hours in the physio clinic trying to regain full mobility. This was the first day I could bend my knee enough to ride the bike

Getting back into training in the Spring of 2008

With Susan Massitti during podium training in Beijing

Competing on rings
during qualification
in Beijing

With my Beijing
teammates Grant,
David, Brandon,
Nathan and Adam

My first Olympic
commentary gig

Kristin and I had a blast on our adventure to Thailand

At the end of a four-hour-long run while training for a marathon with my friend Martin Parnell in 2012

With some of the Kyle Shewfelt Gymnastics team, including Krystal to my right, during the setup of the gym in October 2013.

With Kristin, Nora (6 months) and Cooper in the summer of 2016

Kelli Williams

19

THREE IMPOSSIBLE SCORES

OLYMPIC CHAMPION. TWENTY-FOUR HOURS later, it still didn't feel real. I didn't realize it yet, but the trajectory of my life changed during the two and a half minutes I was up there on the podium.

I didn't really know what to do up on that top step with a crown of olive leaves encircling my head, especially after seeing my face on the jumbotron. *Eeek*, I thought, *look away!* I didn't even notice that the Canadian national anthem faded out before the end because I was too busy trying not to look at myself on the big screen. Kelly, meanwhile, was at the far end of the arena, standing valiantly at attention, a smile of pure joy on his face.

After "O Canada" and a minute of posing for photos with Marian and Jordan, I was taken through the press gauntlet in the mixed zone. One of the first faces I saw was Olympic speedskating legend Catriona Le May Doan, pressed up against the barrier separating journalists and athletes, holding a microphone. *Hey, what's she doing here?* I wondered, and then it dawned that she was there with CBC to interview *me*.

The first thing you do after winning a medal of any colour is media. The second thing is pee into a cup. A doping control officer comes up to you immediately after you compete and follows your every move until nature calls. When you finally have to pee, they watch you do your business, and then the sample is whisked away for testing. Only after that can the celebration begin. Finally, after about an hour, I met my family on the concourse level of the arena and got to put the crown of olive leaves on my mom's head.

My dad enveloped me in a gentle hug. "I will never listen to the Canadian anthem again without thinking about this day," he said. Then, as an afterthought: "I worked a lot of bingos for that gold medal." He had done that and so much more, and so had my mom, but somehow, only as we stood there admiring the ultimate prize around my neck, did it really begin to sink in. I swelled with gratitude for everything they'd given so I could chase my goal. No one wins a gold medal alone.

Diana, camera in hand, snapped a few candid photos, and then I was taken to the International Broadcast Centre for another chat with Brian Williams.

By the time I got back to the Village it was 1 a.m. It was a warm, humid summer night. The Canadian men's baseball team was hanging off their balconies, holding beers they'd somehow gotten ahold of.

"Hey, can I get one of those?" I called out to them.

"For the Olympic gold medallist? Hell yeah!" they hollered back, and tossed me a can.

My teammates were up too. They surrounded me when I got into the apartment, hugging and asking questions and admiring the medal and talking all at the same time. The medal got passed around, and everyone posed for a photo wearing it. I kept thanking everyone, because every single guy had contributed something that had gone into that performance.

"Go write everything down," Dave instructed. "What you ate, what you thought, what you did. You're going to want to remember all of it."

Vault finals were the next day, but I couldn't sleep that night. I went out onto the balcony and sat for a long time, holding my medal and just staring in awe at that piece of gold with a huge satisfied smile on my face. Eventually, I called some friends in Canada. They were ecstatic.

"It's blowing up here," my buddy Jade reported. "All the news channels are replaying it. You won Canada's first gold of the Games. Your face is everywhere!"

I put the olive wreath on my lamp shade and the medal on my bedside table. I kept trying to close my eyes and doze off, but I was too jacked to sleep. Every ten minutes or so, I would sit up, take the medal in my hand and replay the evening in my mind, just to make sure it had all *actually* happened. I had lain in bed for the better part of my life imagining this very moment, and I couldn't quite believe it was real.

"Hello, am I speaking to the Olympic champion?" Mom asked when she called the next morning.

"Why yes, yes you are," I responded cheekily. "Am I speaking to the Olympic champion's mother?"

When I got into the athletes' lounge, I plucked *The Globe and Mail* out of a stack of Canadian newspapers delivered to the team headquarters that morning. Allan Maki, a reporter I'd met in the months leading up to the Games, had written an article about Kelly and me. "A Very Sweet Parting," the headline read. "In his mind's eye, Kelly Manjak can still see a scrawny six-year-old Kyle Shewfelt doing nearly perfect handsprings and showing the flexibility of cooked spaghetti," it began, and suddenly it hit me that this was the last day I would be officially coached by Kelly. Earlier that year, he had decided to move to Ontario right after the Games to be closer to Sue's family while they raised their child. He also wanted to try his hand at coaching women's gymnastics. In that moment, holding that paper, something broke inside me and tears spilled out of my eyes before I had time to think. Right there in the athletes' lounge, I cried like my dog had just died.

After a few minutes, I put on sunglasses to hide my red eyes and headed out. In the stairwell, I ran into Canadian women's head coach Andrei Rodionenko, who stopped to offer his congratulations. Out of respect, I took off my sunglasses and Andrei saw immediately that I was emotional.

"Are you okay?" he asked.

"It's just . . . it's my last day of being coached by Kelly," I confessed. Andrei seemed to understand. Over the years he had seen many Olympic gold medallists in the former Soviet Union and understood the often overwhelming emotions that come with the accomplishment of a long-held goal. As I began to tear up again, he squeezed my shoulders.

"Your coach is a great man," he said over and over. "A great, great man."

● ● ●

I was still in the warm-up gym, waiting for my turn to compete in the vault final, when the carnage began. The finalists up before me were crashing and burning. Athletes were not allowed to do a thirty-second "one-touch" on the equipment in the competition venue before their routines, and they were making big mistakes as a result.

Like podium training, the one-touch is essential for getting a feel for the equipment in the arena. The one-touch gives the athletes a sense of the lighting, TV cameras, and even the crowd right before they compete. The logic behind removing one-touches during apparatus finals was that it made it easier for broadcasters to block out their production timing. Sometimes one-touches would go overtime, which made it challenging for TV producers to determine when to go to commercials. It also eliminated up to four minutes per apparatus which, in theory, made competitions go faster. The bottom line was that the safety of the athletes was sacrificed for TV, and that was evident from the first gymnast to perform.

Alexei Bondarenko was one of the best on the Russian team, but he missed his first vault by a mile, bellyflopping onto the mat in a way that it would hurt to do into a swimming pool. Obviously in pain, he went back down the runway, did his second vault and missed again. He didn't even make it close to landing on his feet, resulting in a score of zero from the judges. Bondarenko came down from the podium and collapsed. His back was broken. He was loaded onto a stretcher and wheeled out of the arena. It was his twenty-sixth birthday.

As I bounced around the warm-up gym staying loose and in my zone, a group of coaches and athletes gathered around the little TV broadcasting what was happening in the arena

100 feet away. From the gasps and oohs emanating from that part of the gym, I gathered that other people were falling too. I wasn't favoured to medal, but I was also sure I could land my two vaults, even without a one-touch. My mind flashed back to the first vault I did in Athens on the first day of training, that textbook one right out of the box. I hadn't needed a one-touch then, and I didn't need one now.

I wasn't one of the top three vaulters in the world. In reality, I was maybe fifth, the place I'd qualified in. Though I trained the double flipping vaults that elicited the biggest gasps from the crowds into the foam pit, I had always opted against competing them on the hard mats. It was essentially a safety issue. About the worst you could do on a Shewfelt gone wrong was damage the ligaments in your knees. Get lost in the middle of a Yurchenko double back and you're literally risking your neck.

So with my vaults, I expected to go out, do my thing, and wave to the crowd one more time. An Olympic champion's curtain call, if you will. And that would be that.

. . .

It felt good to be out in the arena competing again, to revisit the scene of yesterday's triumph. I was still laser focused, yet this time I felt a new sense of freedom. The clouds of expectation had parted and there was nothing left to prove. This one was just for fun.

I did a good first vault and nearly stuck it. I was quick off the table and clean in the air, and the whole thing felt automatic. On my second, I ran fast toward the board and tried to combine an explosive block with a dynamic wrap into the twist. I initiated the twist a little too early, causing me to hop slightly to the right on the landing. That would be a small deduction, but I had fared better than most of the finalists. For a second I was a tad disappointed, knowing I could have done even better, but I quickly let it go. Floor was my event and I had won the ultimate prize. Vault was icing on the cake.

My average score, 9.599, put me in third place with the best in the world still to come. Marian was hands down the most powerful vaulter on the planet. Like mine, his first vault was named after him and it was a doozy: a front handspring followed by two front flips with a half twist at the end. It was the hardest vault in gymnastics and he made it look like a walk in the park. As the rest of the world looked on, Marian glided down the runway and drilled the landing of his Dragulescu. It was one of the most perfect things I'd ever seen in gymnastics.

Welp, I thought, *I'm going to be fourth.*

Marian's second vault was the same as mine: a Kasamatsu with one and a half twists. He was a lot less comfortable with it, but with a stellar 9.9 for his first effort, all he really needed was to stand it up and gold would be his.

But he didn't. As I watched Marian fall on his landing, I heard the collective cry of astonishment from around the arena. I slowly leaned back in my chair, contemplating this Very Unexpected Event.

A second Olympic medal? No way! An hour ago I wouldn't have said it was possible, yet here we were.

Marian was way off after pushing from the table and couldn't get his body around in time to land cleanly. He completed two and a quarter twists, landing with his torso so far backwards and to the side that only someone with his strength could even attempt to keep it on his feet. His upper body whirled around as he tried desperately to save it. The momentum carried him entirely off the landing mat as he lunged, scampered around, and touched his hands to the ground. Given all the deductions, there was no way he could score better than a 9.0 for this effort.

The realization arrived all at once. *I think I just won another Olympic medal.* Bronze on vault after gold on floor. It was my wildest dream come true.

Then Marian's score came up. To everyone's surprise, even with the fall, the average for his two vaults was still higher than mine, putting him into bronze-medal position and bumping me off the podium. I took in the scoreboard, puffed my cheeks and slowly blew out my breath. I didn't know what to think.

In the mixed zone, the journalists huddled around me in a semicircle, all holding portable tape recorders close to my mouth. "I'm proud of what I did today," I told them. "I don't want losing a bronze to be my story of this Games. I want what happened yesterday to be my story." Going back to the Hap adage, I was there to do what I could do and perform my routines. Let the outcomes fall where they may. You hear it again and again from gymnasts: there is only so much you can control.

I thought that was it. I went from the mixed zone into the stands and sat down with my family to watch the rest of the finals. It was just beginning to dawn on me that my Olympics were over. I was contentedly sipping a beer when my phone rang.

It was Nathalie. "Sh-- is exploding," she announced shortly. "Don't move. I'm going to come and get you, okay?"

She was in the grandstands two minutes later. I followed her down several flights of stairs, through the bowels of the Olympic Indoor Hall and outside. A van was parked outside the athlete entrance and Nat hustled me into it like we were making a criminal getaway. Inside sat Kelly, Jean-Paul Caron, the CEO of Gymnastics Canada, and Michael Chambers, the CEO of the Canadian Olympic Committee, all looking like they were in the middle of a very serious meeting. "What's going on?" I asked.

Unbeknownst to me, the Canadian coaches had taken a closer look at the scores of Marian's second vault. It carried a start value of 9.9, the highest possible score Marian could have received for it, had he executed it perfectly.

But Marian hadn't done it perfectly. In fact, he'd racked up so many obvious deductions on the landing—including 0.5 alone for putting his hands down and at least 0.3 for the steps to the side of the mat—that his 9.325 average score for the vault was impossible. It should have been closer to a 9.0 or lower. The judges had gotten it wrong.

Two of them—Jorge Sandoval of Venezuela and Jose Mendez of Portugal—had given Marian a 9.5 for his effort. Mendez had given me 9.45 for the exact same vault with a clearly more controlled landing. Apparently they hadn't seen a fall at all, since the deduction for a fall was 0.5. Xavier Colon, a judge from Puerto Rico, tossed out a 9.45. All three scores were impossibly high. It was elementary school judging. Additionally, Robert Paquin of Canada, the technical assistant responsible for confirming the start value of each vault, had overlooked the fact that Marian did not complete the entirety of his twists and landed with his feet a quarter of a twist short. This should have downgraded the vault's start value to a 9.7, two tenths lower than the 9.9 he was awarded.

Their too-high scores bumped up Marian's two vault average score to 9.612, just a hair higher than my 9.599 average. This wasn't Marian's fault. He knew he had screwed up and you could see it written all over his face. Gold had been within his grasp and he'd let it slip away. He was just a pawn in a very different, very ugly game.

It was corruption, pure and simple. Adrian Stoica, the head of the International Gymnastics Federation's Men's Technical Committee and the top gymnastics official at the Games, was a Romanian. In addition to his role with the International Gymnastics Federation, he was also president of the Romanian Gymnastics Federation. I assume he had decided that his country's gymnast was getting a medal on vault and he had leaned on certain judges to make sure it happened. Maybe it had something to do with the fact that even though we had both scored 9.787 on floor the night before, I won the tie break and Marian had received Olympic silver as a result. We will never know.

When they realized what had happened, Kelly and Tony immediately went to file a protest, asking the judges to review my score in lieu of the inflated score Marian received for his second vault. Sitting at the head table wearing a blazer that bore the Olympic rings, Stoica himself waved Kelly off, barely making eye contact with him and saying nothing.

Kelly appealed to Slava Corn, one of the International Gymnastics Federation's three vice presidents and a fellow Canadian. Slava shrugged helplessly at his protests. "Kelly, do what you gotta do," she told him. Kelly and Tony decided what they had to do was go to the press. I was robbed, they told the journalists in the mixed zone. I should have had bronze, but Stoica had manoeuvred it so his countryman would get a medal no matter what.

I was thunderstruck as I listened to this story. As the van idled outside the venue, Kelly and Jean-Paul said they wanted to continue fighting the ruling, all the way up to the International Court of Arbitration for Sport (CAS) if necessary.

"All right," I said. "Fight this fight. But I don't want my legacy of this Games to be that I lost a bronze. I want it to be that I won a gold." I'm sure I would have felt differently if things hadn't gone my way the night before, but I was scared of the media storm this could cause. I thought back to Canadian figure skaters Jamie Sale and David Pelletier at the 2002 Salt Lake City Olympics, and how their own judging controversy had spiralled into a tornado. I didn't want to be at the centre of that. I felt unprepared to handle myself with confidence when faced with tough questions about the code of points and corruption. I was there to do gymnastics, not to fight a system.

As athletes, we take an oath. We promise that we will respect and abide by the rules which govern the Games, committing ourselves to a sport without doping and drugs, in the true spirit of sportsmanship. Officials take an oath as well. They promise to officiate with complete impartiality, respecting and abiding by the rules which govern them in the true spirit of sportsmanship.

In my opinion, those judges violated their oath. Paquin was responsible for verifying the degree of difficulty of each gymnast's vaults. It appeared that he and the others allowed themselves to be influenced and intimidated by a man who had an agenda to place an athlete from his own country on the podium.

After the Games, there was a reckoning. Sandoval, Mendez, and Colon were sanctioned by the International Gymnastics Federation, as was another official who judged the men's vault final. Paquin was ostracized by the Canadian gymnastics community. He never received a major international judging assignment again.

Three other judges, from the USA, Spain, and Colombia, who had allowed Yang Tae-young's parallel bars score to pass through even though he had been awarded an incorrect start value, were also sanctioned, and three others were suspended for mistakes made during the men's team competition. Despite these sanctions and suspensions, the final results did not change.

Later that year, the International Gymnastics Federation announced it was overhauling the scoring system in artistic gymnastics in order to reward gymnasts who were doing exceptional difficulty. In the future, gymnasts would receive one score for difficulty, which would be open-ended, and one score for execution, which would be capped at 10.0. The difficulty and execution scores would be added together to get the total score for a routine. This system, which is still in place today, was created to ensure that the cheating that took place in Athens never happened again.

I didn't want to harp on a negative that I hadn't created and cloud an otherwise wonderful Olympic experience. I wanted to go and party in the Plaka, to watch other sports and celebrate with my friends, family, and teammates. I wanted to march in the closing ceremony and soak up the rest of the Games.

The Canadian media pitted Marian and me against each other like we were characters in a Marvel comic. He was cast as the villain and I was the good guy. But that wasn't, and isn't, the case at all. He is my friend and someone I deeply admire. He was my rival, not my enemy.

A few months later, I made the decision not to proceed with taking the case to the CAS. I was warned that it would cost Gymnastics Canada upwards of $50,000 in legal fees and travel expenses to try to recover the lost medal, and that my chances of winning were slim. Scoring decisions that were made on the field of play were rarely reversed, especially months after the fact. I thought about how much sports development $50,000 could buy and decided not to pursue it.

Putting the kibosh on the case was ultimately my choice. I didn't want to have to face Stoica and have an "X" on my back if I returned to competition. Several people disagreed strongly and tried to convince me otherwise, but my mind was made up. I just wanted it to go away.

If I could live my life over again, I would have been more aggressive in pursuing justice. It wasn't about the medal. It was about a breach of athlete rights. Olympic-calibre athletes deserve Olympic-calibre judging. Anything less is unacceptable.

20

FAME

THE REST OF THE GAMES PASSED IN A MAGNIFICENT blur. There were long nights spent sipping ouzo in the Plaka, dancing at Heineken House, and skinny dipping in the Aegean Sea, followed by 8 a.m. media calls and a myriad of interviews. Kelly's impending arrival was staying put for the time being, so he decided to remain in Athens for the gymnastics gala and a night of celebrations with our team and friends. When it was time for him to pack his suitcases for the flight back to Canada to start his new life in Ontario, I found him in his room at 2 a.m. as I was coming back from a party. "This isn't goodbye," he said as I sat on his bed helping him fold his T-shirts. "This is just see you later. We came this far together—we are now bonded for the rest of our lives."

Walking into Olympic Stadium at the closing ceremony was a time of celebration. Unlike the opening where the athletes enter by their respective countries, the closing is a free-for-all as every country walks into the stadium united as one. My teammates and I stuck together for the most part and posed for photos with our gymnastics friends from around the world. I brought my medal and passed it around for others to see. The Canadian administrative team snuck in a Canadian flag as big as a swimming pool. As it began to unravel, we ran around under it like kindergym kids under a parachute. With our suitcases already packed and checked in for the early-morning flight, we arrived back at the Village with only two responsibilities: remembering our carry-on luggage and having a good time.

"It was incredible," I raved to Kelly over the phone in the wee hours of the morning. "We had so much fun. I wish you were here!"

"That's great, Kyle," Kelly said warmly. "I'm so glad—" he was interrupted by a small groan somewhere in the distance. "Is everything okay?" I asked. "Uh, I gotta go," Kelly said abruptly and hung up. Turns out Sue's water had broken while Kelly was mid-sentence. Their son Barrett was born a few hours later, on August 30, 2004.

. . .

The Air Canada jet had hardly slid into the gate in Calgary when a smiling hostess approached and asked me to stay on board for just a little while longer. I had been upgraded to first class, so I didn't mind. The next thing I knew, a public relations specialist named Chris Dornan was strolling into the plane's cabin.

"Have you brushed your teeth?" he asked, skipping over hello.

"Um . . . no," I admitted. I'd had a late final night in the Olympic Village, followed by a ten-hour flight from Athens to Montreal, where we missed our connection and had to hang around the airport an extra three hours. I couldn't wait to get home and crash into bed. Personal hygiene was the last thing on my mind.

"You might want to do that," Chris said. "There are a few people waiting outside. You're going to be smiling a lot."

There was a flood of people crowded around the arrivals gate, all craning for a glimpse of a newly minted Olympic champion. Among them was my extended family, many of whom had driven from all across Western Canada to be there. The second I walked into the terminal, the crowd broke into an enormous round of applause and cheers. Flashbulbs went off and cameras rolled. Gymnastics fans waved handmade signs as I made my way toward my family.

That was the beginning. I had been so focused on the Olympics that I hadn't really thought about what would happen afterward. I got that my life had changed, but only as I sat on the balcony that night with the medal in my hands staring off at the lights in the Village did I really begin to consider the possibilities.

Before leaving Athens, I had signed with a sports marketing agency who had assigned a cheerful woman named Michelle Comeau to be my manager. Michelle mapped out a plan for handling life after Olympic gold and filtered through the requests that came in. Everyone kept telling me that there was only a small window of time to capitalize on my success. There were *so* many opportunities to choose from: keynote addresses, appearances, autograph sessions, gymnastics shows, red-carpet events, dinners, charity galas, golf tournaments, award banquets, school visits, fundraisers—you name it and my invitations were in the mail.

A couple days later I was flown by private helicopter to Calgary's Canada Olympic Park for a massive celebration ceremony with the mayor and other dignitaries. Medal around my neck, I made the rounds of the morning shows, recounting my story and reliving the routine over and over. The excitement was non-stop and the impact extended beyond my city. I had heard that the phones of gymnastics clubs across the nation had been ringing off the hook with eager parents wanting to get their children enrolled in gymnastics.

The opportunities came fast and thick. One day I would be spending the day on a Dreams Take Flight trip to Disneyland with special needs children and their families, and another I was marshal of a parade. I also signed a sponsorship deal with Bell Canada, which would allow me to focus solely on my training until the 2008 Olympics if I ended up pursuing it.

While the attention flooded in, I had one caveat. In sixteen years of training, I had never had a one-week, all-inclusive vacation. After Athens, I just wanted to go away and lounge by the pool for a few days with a good book and a bottomless bottle of Corona. Michelle bent my schedule to make it happen. I booked tickets to Mexico and Melissa and I jetted off two days later.

When we came back, I found myself doing keynote speeches at $10,000 a pop. I was named the athlete of the year here, there, and everywhere. The Lionel Conacher Award, won multiple times by the great Wayne Gretzky, went to me in 2004. I could hardly believe it.

In December, I attended a Special Olympics gala in Toronto and was immediately hooked. The organization's mandate of providing a safe and inclusive space for those with an intellectual disability to participate in sport aligned with my values. I learned that the athletes often face discrimination and isolation because of their differences, just as I had for being a male gymnast at the sport school. I remembered the promise I made to myself back then: if there was ever an opportunity to be involved in an organization that promoted inclusive values, I would be on board. Special Olympics was it. Spending time with the athletes made me joyful, especially when they showed off their collections of medals and reminded me that I *only* had one!

Embarrassingly, at twenty-two years old, what I didn't have at all was a high school diploma. Ironically, the reason revolved around physical education. In 2001, the Alberta government's Minister of Education denied my request for Grade 11 and 12 physical education credits, all I needed to complete the graduation requirements. "P.E. consists of more than one activity, and I am not able to grant any credits based solely on your gymnastics participation," the minister had written in a refusal letter.

I was dumbfounded. Since there was no way I could take P.E. classes on top of my training regime, I put the diploma on the back burner. My poor mother didn't forget about it, and when she met the newest principal of the National Sport School at a conference, she told him my story. He agreed to grant me the credits and I became an official graduate of the NSS. As a token of my appreciation, I delivered that year's graduation keynote address.

There were some, um, *unusual* experiences too. At one afterparty, some guy came up out of the blue and *licked* the medal around my neck. "Dude!" I cried. "Do you have any idea how many people have been touching that?" At a fundraising dinner, a guest who had had too much red wine accidentally slid the medal's ribbon through his gravy. I was not pleased and glared at him from across the table for the rest of the night.

After a while it was like I'd wandered into a pinball machine and was being flung wildly from one place to another. On airplanes, I'd be getting seated and suddenly a flight attendant would appear and tell me I'd been bumped up to first. I got really good at talking to strangers around random dinner tables. People comped my meals in restaurants or came up and asked to take photos. In Calgary, I'd go to the grocery store and people would point and stare at me as I picked out fruit in the produce section.

I was everywhere and doing everything because I felt like that's what I had to do to capitalize on my hard-earned success. I obliged nearly everyone who wanted an autograph, a picture, or a high-five. I was so grateful to have earned such acclaim, but quickly realized that you don't get much rest when you have to be on all the time. Finding five-minute pockets of solitude became a very important ritual for my mental health.

· · ·

I was in the changing room after a hot yoga class in Calgary one night when an older man caught sight of the Olympic rings tattoo on my shoulder blade. "What's the tattoo for?" he asked.

"I'm a gymnast," I said, and the man's eyes lit up. "Are you going to be the next Kyle Shewfelt?"

I kind of laughed. "Actually, I am Kyle Shewfelt."

The man looked embarrassed. "Oh, I'm so sorry!" he said. "I didn't recognize you. Your hair is longer and curly now, and you're so much shorter in person!" That was one of the things people would always say when they met me: "Holy cow, you're short!"

It's true: I'm 5'5" (1.65 metres), but on TV I looked six feet tall. They say the camera adds ten pounds, but I'm convinced it also adds at least six inches to your height.

· · ·

The oddity of my name but not my face being recognized stayed with me as I drove home from the hot yoga studio. The Olympic success had made me a brand—Kyle Shewfelt, the gymnast—but who was *I?* How strange it was to wonder where I fit into the brand I had created just by being me and doing the sport I loved.

In the midst of all this, I bought my first home in Calgary. It was a suburban cookie-cutter two-storey with brown stucco and black trim and it was close to the airport, which was a good thing because Melissa and I were there often. She had started a job as a flight attendant and I was on the road, sometimes five days a week, for months. Melissa would accompany me whenever she could, and her employee flight benefits definitely came in handy. I said yes to nearly everything I was offered because I didn't want to miss out on anything or disappoint anyone. Michelle arranged the logistics and all I had to do was show up for the flight. I saw more of Vancouver, Toronto, Ottawa, and small towns across Alberta than I ever had before and I would often tack on a quick visit with Kelly, Sue, and their new bundle of joy when I found myself out on the eastern side of the country.

All the travelling left no time for training apart from some handstand push-ups in hotel rooms. I lost a lot of muscle mass riding the Olympic wave. When I ran into Tony at a Salute to Olympians dinner, he took one look at me and exclaimed, "Man, where did your biceps vanish to?" With a wink, he added, "I think it might be time for some rope climbs . . ."

By the end of November and three months entirely away from the gym, I decided I should focus more on a return to training. That meant finding a new coach and a new facility, since Altadore now lacked a high-level men's coach.

The most logical solution lay with Tony at the U of C. I met with him and his star pupil Nathan Gafuik, who had been the Olympic team alternate, and we agreed that I would train there in the future. I had thought hard and mapped out a few things I wanted when it came to my new training situation. Firstly, I wanted to remain in Calgary. I couldn't imagine uprooting my life and leaving all my family and friends behind to train elsewhere. I also knew that a change of training venue would be a good thing for me in this next phase of my career. Lastly, I wanted to stop training pommel horse and parallel bars and focus on my preferred events only. Even though rings wasn't my strongest apparatus, I felt that I could contribute a solid backup score for the team if needed, so I opted to continue training it as well.

Tony and I had developed a mutual respect for each other, and he had softened a lot since the days of physical-abilities testing. We quickly connected and found a good groove. But even as I settled into my new situation, it was hard to get back to anything serious when I was at the gym one day and then gone doing appearances for the next five.

My intention was to compete at the 2005 Canadian Championships in British Columbia, but another wave of opportunities slowed my progress. Nationals, then Worlds, came and went. I didn't feel too worried; there were almost three years until the 2008 Olympics in Beijing. I had plenty of time to get myself back on track.

. . .

Then, all of a sudden, it was gone.

I was driving home from the gym one night when it hit me: my passion for gymnastics—what had driven me for nearly my entire lifetime—was *gone*. Poof.

I tore into the house and put on the 2004 Olympic tape. I watched the routine that had changed my life . . . and couldn't imagine myself doing it again. It was as if the compartment inside of my brain that was in charge of dispensing motivation was empty. Hollow. *Nothing*.

It was around this time Hap invited me to be a part of a sport neuroscience research project that used an fMRI (functional magnetic resonance imaging) machine to look at how an athlete's brain processes the video replay of personal success or failure. The research project didn't make a lick of sense to me, but I respected Hap and so flew to Vancouver and let them put electrodes all over me as I lay in an fMRI machine to be monitored. For several minutes, I watched my 2004 Olympic floor routine and felt joy and sadness equally flowing through me as if my emotions were a lava lamp.

The results, Hap explained afterwards, revealed that my neural response to watching my performance was similar to the response of a person who was depressed. As I'd discovered in 2000, after the excitement of the Games dissipates, your life recalibrates and you begin wondering what's next. I didn't know. For the first time in more than a decade, I wasn't driving toward something concrete. *Hadn't I accomplished my ultimate goal? Wasn't this supposed to make me the happiest person on the planet for all of eternity? Why was I starting to feel let down again?*

. . .

The school principal gestured toward me, eyes sparkling and a glowing smile on her face. "Please give a warm welcome to Olympic gold medallist Kyle Shewfelt!" she exclaimed to the assembled students.

Three hundred pairs of eyes swivelled toward me as I walked out on my hands to the centre of the stage. "Hi!" I said, still upside down. The kids burst into approving giggles. I stepped out of the handstand and launched into my presentation. My motivational talks came to touch on everything I stood for, beginning with the importance of having a big dream and finding joy in what you do, leading to how having goals encouraged commitment, drive and purpose—all things I didn't really feel anymore.

What a hypocrite you are, I thought. Here I was talking to school kids about direction and drive when I didn't have them anymore. I had spent my whole life chasing one dream, and now that it had become a reality, I had no idea what to do. Watching that routine in the fMRI machine made me long for the feeling I had on that day in Athens when I knew exactly what I wanted and I was going after it. Try as I might, I couldn't pinpoint what came next and it was hugely confusing.

I wasn't sure if I wanted to continue with gymnastics.
"Sometimes I am relieved that I did it and I am done," I wrote
in my journal. After I wrote that, I sat back and pondered the
words on the page. Could I continue with the sport? Or was it
time to move on?

· · ·

Scowling and snapping my gum, I slouched through the gym
in a red and white tracksuit. When I got to the edge of the foam
pit, I casually flipped into it with my hands in my pockets. *I
don't give a f---*, my attitude seemed to say. At least, that's what
I was going for.

"Good!" Uldi called from behind the camera. My old friend
had joined Cirque du Soleil after the 2002 Worlds and now he
was back in Canada with a big new project. Uldi was starring in
a film about a man's traumatic childhood in gymnastics with an
abusive coach, which resurfaces when he moves to Canada and
becomes a mentor to a talented but moody teenage gymnast.
The plot sounded eerily familiar.

I must have really made an impression on him during our
training days, because when they needed to cast the talented but
moody teenager, Uldi called me up right away. I wanted to pay it
forward, so I agreed to be involved. Uldi had made gymnastics
fun during that challenging time when Kelly and I were not
seeing eye to eye and the goal had seemed so far away. I felt it
was my turn to help Uldi bring *his* vision to life.

White Palms was directed by Uldi's brother Szabolcs Hajdu,
and we filmed in both Calgary and Budapest. In Calgary, we filmed
scenes at Altadore, and the only time we could get the entire gym

to ourselves was from 9 p.m. to 9 a.m., meaning I had to perform tumbling passes and release moves in the middle of the night.

In Hungary, I had the chance to catch up with Marian, who was also cast as a gymnast. One day at lunch, out of the blue, he asked, "How much did you make from your government for winning gold in Athens? I heard it was $500,000!"

I burst out laughing. "That would have been great," I said truthfully, "but try something more like $5,000." At the time, the Canadian government had an incentive program in place called the Canadian Recognition Support Program, which rewarded those who placed in the top five at a world championships or Olympic Games with a $5,000 cheque. In Romania, by contrast, a gold was reportedly rewarded with $55,000 Euros (roughly $80,000 Canadian). The package was also rumoured to include a brand-new car and a pension for life.

Marian looked at me as though I'd sprouted a second head. "Five thousand?!" he exclaimed. "Like, a five with *only* three zeros? Then why the hell did you do it?"

"I love gymnastics," I said simply. "And it was my dream." Just saying it helped me remember: I *did* love the sport, even if I didn't love the time I was going through right then.

Marian shook his head slowly, still looking shocked. "You're a crazy man," he finally said.

• • •

Canadian figure skating legend Elvis Stojko and I took one look at the glittery red, white, and blue costumes we'd been given to wear for the Hilton Family Skating and Gymnastics Spectacular being taped in Atlanta and burst out laughing.

"Do you think we should let them know we're from Canada?" Elvis whispered. It was an American TV production, which meant that it involved star-spangled singlets, even for the two Canadian dudes.

The concept was to have stars show off routines and skills, but also to mix up the format. Guys were paired with girls for duo numbers, and skaters would glide alongside gymnasts. It was also a chance for everybody to cut loose and have some fun. I was paired with Dominique Moceanu for a tango routine choreographed by Adriana Pop, a famous Romanian gymnastics choreographer.

During the practice session, the other guys tumbling in the show, including Paul Hamm and his twin brother Morgan, kept ripping off easy double layouts. I had originally planned to do a full twisting double back, a slightly easier tumbling pass that I could do in my sleep, but when I saw Paul and Morgan's double layouts, a little competitive flame ignited in my belly. I decided on the spot that if they were doing double layouts, then so would I.

I should add that the double layout has never really been my skill. Also, that we were performing in an ice rink. The floor mat, set up over the icy surface, gave next to nothing on takeoff. It would be fine, I figured. It wasn't. During the filming, I landed short and crunched my foot. For the sake of the cameras I hobbled through the rest of the routine, but afterward I was in so much pain that I couldn't do my solo floor routine.

To celebrate the end of the taping, there was a wrap party at the hotel where everyone was staying. I stayed late, hanging in the bar with old and new friends and ignoring my throbbing foot, which somehow seemed less painful as the night went on.

I talked a lot with Dominique that night, opening up about the whirlwind of life after winning the Olympics. Dominique was one of the few people who could understand what it was like: as the youngest member of the "Magnificent Seven" American women's team that won gold in Atlanta in 1996, she and her teammates had toured their country like rock stars afterward. After a while, though, she too had begun feeling lost.

"It's definitely intense," she said with a sympathetic smile. "There are all of these external demands on your time and you can end up feeling like you have no control over your life."

"You know what freaks me out, though?" I said. "Before the Olympics I was so focused and so driven, and now I just don't really feel any motivation or momentum."

"And you're not going to," she said, "until you really make the commitment to training again. Once you buckle down, you'll be surprised at how much clearer things seem."

I got back to my room as the sun was rising and fell into bed. I crashed for about an hour before getting up and going to the airport, sleepwalking through check-in and boarding. By the time the plane took off, I was nestled into my seat, dead to the world.

When I came to a few hours later, my foot felt like it had been run over by a cement truck. *How the hell did I not feel this before?* I wondered briefly. For the first time, I realized that something might really be wrong with it. During the layover in Denver, I called the Canadian Sport Centre. "I need an X-ray right away when I land in Calgary," I said. Then I hobbled off to find a row of chairs so I could put my foot up.

Everything quickly came into focus when I learned the diagnosis: a fractured bone in my right foot. It was time to get serious.

21

HEAVY MEDAL

THE COLD, STARK FEAR HAD MY STOMACH IN KNOTS.
Once again, I was standing in the corner of the floor at the
World Championships, and once again the little voice in my
head was reminding me of my duties.

Mostly, it repeated one thing: *Don't screw up. You know
what's riding on this.*

I did know—and it was a lot more than just a world medal.

Winning Olympic gold changes a person's life—the last
eighteen months had taught me that over and over. What I didn't
realize so much before going back to training was that it can also
change the lives of a person's teammates. The main difference
is the moola.

Funding in Canadian sport has always been tied to
the government. Canadian federations are funded by an
organization called Sport Canada, rather than big corporations
like Nike or Visa. In the lead-up to the 2010 Winter Olympics
in Vancouver, the government, always in limited funds, had to
choose where to invest its cash. To figure out where, it created
an organization called Own the Podium, which looked around

and identified certain athletes and sports as having "high performance potential," i.e., a real chance to win a medal at upcoming Games.

And since Athens, men's gymnastics was suddenly considered high performance potential, and thereby eligible for funding from Own the Podium. In other words, the men's program had won a modest jackpot. Our resources, which had once been close to nothing, exploded overnight. Suddenly, we had access to sports doctors we'd never been able to see before. We could get massages with licensed massage therapists and private sessions with personal trainers. Instead of driving across Calgary to go to the chiropractor, one came to the gym and set up a table just off the side of the floor.

There was travel, too. Thanks to the newfound resources, our whole team was able to do more training camps. We did multiple camps at the National Sports Training Centre in Beijing, getting ourselves used to a long flight followed by a hard workout, because we knew that would be the drill in Beijing in 2008. We got to take advantage of time in China, going out to markets and sampling a lot of what the city had to offer. That was strategic too. If we got to be tourists now, the coaches thought, it would be out of our system by the time the Games rolled around, leaving us completely focused on the Olympics.

We also got new, state-of-the-art equipment. I arrived at the U of C one day to find a new European Spieth brand of floor being installed in the centre of the gym. Euro Spieth would be the official equipment supplier for the 2007 World Championships in Stuttgart, Germany, which doubled as the Olympic team qualifier. Tony and I wanted us all to train on the same thing we'd perform on in Stuttgart, so we got one. That would have been unheard of only two years earlier.

It was a good thing we were getting such good care, because with the new open-ended scoring system, gymnastics had become much harder.

The coaches and gymnasts read over the new code of points and quickly realized one thing: the way to get a big score was to compete extremely difficult skills. The risks, including injury, were significantly increased, but for the guys who could master a hugely difficult set and do it without giving away much in execution, the potential rewards were huge.

Everyone upped their game. I changed my opening tumbling pass from the four rebounding skills to a splashy Arabian double front pike and began training the same pass in a straight body position, making an already hard skill even more difficult. I completely changed the construction of my routine, just to make sure I was racking up enough difficulty points to stay in contention.

I still ended with the double double. The difference here was that I now executed *four* difficult tumbling passes before it, versus just two in Athens. It required a lot more endurance, and my lungs were always screaming at me beforehand. If you wanted to be near the top, it was what you had to do. And in 2006, it was working for me—when I wasn't terrified of making a mistake.

It's so much easier to be the hunter. To see the goal flashing right in front of you and to drive straight toward it with everything you have. And then you get it and it's great, for a while. But then you begin thinking that a gymnast is only as good as his or her last competition. And you realize that at the next competition, everyone is going to be gunning for you and you'll have to be even better than ever.

When you've put a lifetime into one Olympic moment, thinking that the next time you go out on the floor you're going to have to be even better is a hellish prospect. It made me afraid to compete again. *What will people think if I make a mistake?* The thought began to plague me and my anxiety seemed to manifest itself in my Achilles tendons, which felt like they might explode on any given takeoff.

Added to that stress was the pressure of understanding the business side of what was going on here. Before the 2006 World Championships in Aarhus, I was well aware that if the Canadian men's team came home empty-handed, our funding would likely be reduced. That would mean fewer training camps, less in the way of treatment and fewer resources for our very talented team. Own the Podium's expectations hung over all of us, and as I stood preparing to compete in the floor final, I knew it ultimately came down to me.

Our team had had a breakthrough performance in the qualification round in Denmark and moved into our first-ever team final ranked in fifth position. Sasha and Richard were now retired, but that opened the door for a new generation of talented Canadian gymnasts to take centre stage. There was my new training mate Nathan, who was great on high bar and even better at flirting with the Italian women's team out of our hotel room window. There was Adam, who had continued to improve since Athens and was equally strong across all six events. Finally, there was the one whom I always felt breathing down my neck: Brandon O'Neill, a ginger-haired firecracker from Edmonton who had won the 2005 World Championship silver medal on floor. He kept me on my toes.

We were a well-balanced bunch, rounded out by veterans Dave and Ken. Our alternate was Grant, which showed the depth amongst our team.

In the team final, we placed a respectable sixth. It was an impressive jump from our previous world team ranking of ninth in 2003, but not enough to convince Own the Podium that we were a medal threat as a team at the next Olympics. Medals spoke. Sixth place finishes, as proud as they made us feel, weren't enough to earn maximum funding dollars.

If the Canadian men came away without a medal at this World Championships, we'd be on the funding bubble. Adam and Nathan had qualified for the all-around final and finished ninth and seventeenth, respectively. As the only Canadian man to have made an individual event final, I approached my floor routine with my tail between my legs. Warrior mode seemed like long ago.

The vocal track in the back of my mind repeated *Don't screw up.*

Don't screw up.

This was new, and the polar opposite of the "make it happen" mindset I faced the Olympic final with just two years prior. In Athens, it was about the performance and going after it. Here it was about the final placement and trying not to make a mistake. This shift in perspective made me feel numb. It was like a dark cloud was hanging over my head, similar to the dreary grey skies that existed outside in Aarhus during much of that World Championships. The whole time I knew it was wrong and shouldn't have been thinking it, but I couldn't seem to gain control of my thoughts. The negative self-talk swirled and I was left as an observer.

I made a major error on my new first tumbling pass, a very large step back, and it sprung me awake. Our thoughts become our actions. Relief washed through my veins when I landed the final tumbling run and acknowledged the judges. I ran off the floor as though it were chasing me. All I could think was *Thank God that's over.*

I won bronze behind Diego Hypolito and Marian. It wasn't the result I would have preferred, but after the roller coaster of the past two years I could be content with it. Canada had a medal and our funding would stay intact.

What I realize now is that after 2004, I had lost the sense of the athlete who loved the chase. I no longer saw what the sport had to offer and instead I started to focus on everything my teammates and I had to lose . . . and it almost tore me apart.

In 2004 I had been free and charging. By 2006, I was trapped by my own expectations. I shrugged it off—what else could I do?—and told myself that 2007 would be better. Something had to give.

22

BROKEN LEGS

AND THEN SOMETHING DID GIVE: MY LEGS.

The German doctors wanted to do surgery as soon as possible, but something made me insist that we wait. Instead of gowning up and wheeling me into an operating room, Susan, the team's physical therapist, sent the MRI results and images to Dr. Nick Mohtadi, a Canadian team surgeon in Calgary. Dr. Mohtadi reviewed the X-rays and advised against operating right away.

"I'm seeing some potential ligament damage that wasn't mentioned in the initial diagnosis, so I want to see him in person before a surgical plan is laid out," he told Susan. He also wanted an opportunity to review the images with his colleagues to ensure nothing was overlooked. The surgery would be invasive, and after much consultation, everyone thought it would be best for me to have the operation and to recover at home in Calgary.

Sleep that first night was impossible. I lay in bed with two huge navy-blue braces straightening my legs, feeling the blood flowing through them but unable to move. The pain levels went up and down, up and down.

At the hospital, a nurse had come in with a big plastic jar. "For you," she said, holding it out.

I looked at it blankly. "What am I supposed to do with it?"

"You urinate in it," she said. Seeing the look on my face, she added hastily, "If you don't use it, we will have to put a catheter in." Mystified, I looked at Susan, who helpfully explained what a catheter was. Given the option of peeing in a jar or having a tube inserted into my unmentionable, I reluctantly accepted the jar. Later, a rush of stubbornness came over me and, with help, I was able to make it to the bathroom. The jar now sat on my bedside table, a reminder that I was completely dependent on other people to get even the most private of tasks done.

I'm never using that thing, I vowed. *Furthermore, someday I'm going to drink margaritas out of it.*

As the hours wore on, I came to grips with the reality of the situation. I was injured—very injured—and for the moment there was nothing I could do except begin physical therapy and try to rest. But I couldn't stop thinking about how this turn of events was going to affect our team, which needed a top-twelve finish at these World Championships to qualify to Beijing. I felt a massive amount of fear and guilt. *If Canada doesn't qualify for the Games,* I thought, *it will be all my fault.*

If I couldn't physically contribute on the apparatus, I wanted to show the guys that I was still as all in as I could possibly be. The thought of heading back to Calgary with so many question marks in the air didn't sit right. I didn't want to read the final results on the internet; I wanted to be with them at every training session and on the sidelines during the competition, offering the loudest cheers. So I decided to stay until the qualification round was over. That way I could bring the team strength, even if I couldn't perform. I would stay and be cheerful, at least on the outside. Once I'd settled that in my head, I slid into a semi-conscious snooze.

I wasn't prepared for what I saw when Susan un-Velcroed the braces the next morning. My legs were swollen from heel to hip, with green, purple, and yellow bruises puckering the landscape. "Ew!" I yelped as Susan surveyed the damage with an experienced eye. "Broken blood vessels, from the impact," she said, quickly re-splinting them. In the wheelchair, both my legs stuck straight out in front of me. Susan pulled a pair of gloves out of her backpack and handed them to me. "I bought these for you. They'll help you get grip while you wheel around," she said.

Each morning for the next several days, Susan got me situated and worked on my legs, taping them with blue kinesiotherapy tape to help increase blood flow. She also administered a daily dose of a blood thinner to make sure clots didn't develop in my legs. I hoped the anticoagulant would come in pill form. It didn't.

"What are you doing?" I asked nervously the first time I saw her preparing the syringe.

"I have to give this to you as a shot," she replied, flicking the needle lightly. "In your stomach. Lift up your shirt, all right?"

"How many times are you going to have to do that?"

"Every morning, Kyle. It's necessary."

Ugh.

Since doing gymnastics was out, I assumed the role of team bag boy. Everyone slung their gym bags over my wheelchair as we got into the gym, and I'd manage them while they worked out. At the gym, I'd peel myself out of the wheelchair and make my way to the edge of the floor, where I would sit with an electrostimulation machine hooked up to my thighs. We were trying to head off the atrophy as much as possible. Afterwards, Susan and I often set out to see Stuttgart's city parks. Learning to do a wheelie in the chair wasn't nearly as good as competing at Worlds, but it did lift my spirits a little.

The braces were so unwieldy that I had my own row of seats on the shuttle buses that scooted us between the hotel and the gyms. Coaches from all over the world worked together to lift me on and off the buses. Everywhere I went, people stared. Some whispered and pointed. Others came up to ask what happened. When we ran into the American women's team coming out of the training hall one day, they all looked at me with their eyes bugging out of their heads. "Oh my God, Kyle, what the hell did you do?" team captain Alicia Sacramone finally blurted out.

"Bad landing," I said casually, raising my palms in the air. The Americans exchanged incredulous looks, but before we could really get into a discussion on the dangers of our sport, U.S. national team coordinator Martha Karolyi intervened.

"Right girls, ve must get going, ve'll be late for ze bus!" she trilled in her thick Romanian accent, clapping her hands. The American team just kept staring at me. Martha cast a dismissive look at me in my wheelchair. "Oooookay, bye-bye now," she said, gently squeezing the back of Shawn Johnson's neck and funnelling the group away.

When competition day came, the guys got it done. The team—Dave, Grant, Nathan, Brandon, Ken, and Casey—stepped up to the plate and delivered an eleventh-place finish, qualifying a full Canadian team for the second consecutive Games. During the meet, I cheered as loud as I could and delivered high-fives from the sideline. When the results became official, I grinned from ear to ear for the first time in days.

. . .

The airport was a farce.

There I was in my wheelchair, braced legs splayed out as usual. There Susan was at the check-in desk, arguing with the Air Canada gate agent, making a case for why I shouldn't have to pass the next ten hours in coach.

"You are a *Canadian Olympic Team sponsor,*" she said through clenched teeth, enunciating the words slowly and deliberately. "You have an injured *Olympic champion* here. Both of his *legs* are *broken*. He's flying home to have *surgery*. And you won't put him in first class?! Boy, wait until the press gets ahold of that!"

Susan finally took out her credit card and was trying to pay for my upgrade herself. She stood at the counter brandishing it and glaring while I sat quietly off to the side in my wheelchair, thinking that my redheaded guardian angel had morphed into a red-faced guardian badass.

Finally the gate agent relented and let me into first class, where I spent the flight to Calgary as comfortable as it was possible to be in my condition. Susan was stuck back in coach. They let her into the front of the plane only so she could help me go to the bathroom and rub my legs to keep the blood flowing. I had to scoot myself across the floor in an L-sit position and hoist myself up onto the toilet seat in order to use the can.

"I never thought I'd see someone touch the bathroom floor of an airplane," the flight attendant said ruefully as she handed me a few packs of wet wipes, the look on her face reflecting compassion and disgust in roughly equal measures. She and Susan stood guard at the door, since my extended legs kept it from closing.

• • •

I had never been so glad to see my old room. It was just as I had left it nearly three years earlier, down to the blue walls, blue comforter, and blue carpet. Melissa picked me up from the airport and drove me to my parents' house. I was very relieved to see her, and after her initial shock at my bruised and atrophied legs, we just laughed about the absurdity of it all. We'd been taking a break in our relationship because, quite frankly, preparation for a big competition is often selfish and I didn't have much else to give. But when I called and told her what had happened, she dropped everything to be by my side. During the next few weeks, she stayed right there, tending to me and driving me to all my appointments. My family called her Nurse Nightingale. I'll never forget her selflessness.

I received so much support during this time, and not just from Melissa, my family, and close friends. Even Canadian celebrities reached out to offer their support. Comedian Rick Mercer made me laugh by sending a sympathy email whose subject line was a single four-letter word that started with an "F."

My dad had gone to a medical supply store and come home with a rented wheelchair and a portable ramp so I wouldn't have to be carried up the front steps and, the next morning, Scott wheeled me down the ramp and heaved me into the car.

• • •

I lay on a gurney while Dr. Mohtadi took a black marker and X-ed the places where he would make incisions. The main diagnosis was displaced tibial fractures, accompanied by some residual effects caused by the impact. Most of the impact of the landing had been absorbed by my left leg, a hazard when you twist to the left. It had sustained the brunt of the damage. A plate and four screws were to be inserted into my left knee, while my right would escape with a single screw. Dr. Mohtadi would remove bone chips and repair a severely stretched LCL (lateral collateral ligament) on the left side, and Humpty Dumpty Shewfelt would be put back together again.

I looked away as the IV went into my arm. Susan was there to observe the surgery and offered to hold my hand. For the first thirty seconds or so, the anaesthetic had no effect. *I'm going to fight this*, I thought as my mind began wandering hazily. *I'm going to see if I can stay awake.* An image of the gym flicked into my head. Looking at the mats and equipment was like looking at a memory of my childhood home. My eyes suddenly felt heavy. *I'm going to come back*, I thought. *To prove . . .*

That's about when I lost consciousness.

. . .

I felt like a plant that had been left out in the desert for days. Never had my whole body felt so thirsty and dry.

"Water," I managed to croak. "Please, water. I'm so thirsty."

The night was fuzzy. At some point, another plastic pee jar appeared and this time I didn't argue. Unfortunately, not much made it into the jar as I peed all over myself, so the nurses had to come back in and change my gown and the sheets. Then I wanted toast. I moaned for toast. Someone brought in a plate of whole-wheat toast with butter on it. I scarfed it down and felt more grateful than I ever had for anything.

The nurses wanted to give me morphine to ease the pain in my legs that first night. I didn't want it and said so.

"We suggest you take it," they responded dryly. I shook my head. No. I wanted to own my pain. That's what gymnasts did.

Gone were the original braces from Stuttgart. My legs were encased in even larger, bulky black plastic braces that ran from thigh to mid-calf. They were locked at a slightly bent angle and it felt like an army of invisible gremlins were busy driving very real daggers into them. The sensation was unbearable.

"Kyle, are you sure you don't want any morphine?" a voice from far off asked again. I don't remember much of the night after that, but after what seemed like a very long time, I did manage to sleep.

Years later, I was sitting in a restaurant in Calgary when a woman approached my table. "You're Kyle Shewfelt, aren't you?" she asked. I nodded. "I was one of the nurses who took care of you the night after your operation," she said. "You were a handful. Did you know that at first you didn't want the morphine, but we gave it to you anyway? After that you were much easier to handle."

. . .

I had become a man-infant. Once home, I couldn't do anything—and I mean *anything*—without someone else's help. Having one busted leg would have been horrible but manageable. Two was just debilitating. I was confined to my bed and used a walker to get from my bedroom to the bathroom. I was told that feather weight on the tips of my toes would help promote healing. I'll never forget the clip-clopping sound of the walker as I made my way down the hardwood hallway. I needed help getting a glass of water, making a meal, even getting into bed. Bathing was particularly challenging and my parents saw parts of me that they hadn't seen since I was about five. My room was a disaster. "I can make a lovely mess, but I have to leave it there until someone else can clean it up," I wrote on my blog.

Worst of all was the pain. As a gymnast, I had been taught that pain is progress. I had been conditioned to "work through the pain." At first, I thought resisting morphine and other pain medications made me strong. It actually made me miserable, and I, in turn, made everybody else miserable. Eventually I relented, and Percocet and Tylenol 3s became an every-four-hour snack.

My mom and Melissa packed plastic bags full of ice onto my legs, which felt like they'd swollen to ten times their normal size. At night, I had panic-inducing flashbacks of the accident, reliving the impact and the searing pain. It was so bad that I'd wake up sweating and screaming and either my mom or Melissa would run in to see what was wrong. "My legs!" I'd sob, contorted with pain.

When I was more lucid, I moaned about how bad I was at relaxing. "Wasting time like this makes me feel so lazy," I whined. "My mind is melting from just sitting and watching TV all day."

"Look," Melissa said, "I know you think you always need to be strong, but right now you need to *not* be strong, okay? You're going to need to be strong later. And I know you think you aren't doing anything, but by doing nothing, you're actually doing something extremely important: you're healing. And you can't begin to accomplish anything until you've healed."

As the days passed, the muscle tone in my legs melted away. The first time I took the braces off for ten minutes of reprieve, my flabby calves dangled and swung from side to side. The yellow from the iodine and the black marking from where the surgeons had cut hadn't rubbed away. They stank like a locker room. I lay in bed and looked at them and felt helpless. I had been in such good shape. And now? Nothing.

It seemed like so long ago that I flipped and twisted through the air, confident and precise. I used to lie in bed thinking about my routines and sticking my landings. Everything from that time seemed free and easy and very long ago.

"It's so funny how perspective and goals can change so much in a single moment," I wrote on my blog. "One month ago I was dreaming of nailing my routines at Worlds, now I am dreaming about just being able to walk."

Where in the world, I wondered as I closed the laptop and leaned back on my pillows, *do I go from here?*

23

THE POOL

WHAT GETS GLOSSED OVER ABOUT RECOVERY is that it takes forever. It is slow and boring and at times deeply frustrating, and the first part—the weeks where you sit around doing nothing waiting for your bones to grow back together—is the worst of all. You keep wondering if there is something you can do, and the answer is no. There is nothing you can do. As someone accustomed to having total control over their body, it is terrible.

Since you have nowhere to go and nothing to do, you spend a lot of time in your own head, reliving the moment of the injury and wondering if there was anything you could have done to prevent it. I realized that I was confident in my decision to attempt the Tamayo on that day, and I didn't have any regrets, so I kept circling back to the notion that perhaps this was meant to be. But what, exactly, was fate trying to say? Was there something I was supposed to learn from this experience?

A week after my surgery, we held a press conference at the Olympic Oval. As I was wheeled up to the podium, my legs still in their braces and still sticking straight out in front of me, an explosion of flashbulbs popped in my face. As Dr. Mohtadi and Tony and I answered the eager questions from the media, it dawned on me how intensely Canadians had been following my story. I realized something else, too: this wasn't just about me and my goal of making it back to the Olympics. This was also about the attitude I approached this comeback with. Others were looking in.

At first, all I could really do was show up at the university and go through the motions of basic physical therapy, which involved Susan rubbing her fingers up and down the incisions on my knees, trying to stimulate the nerve endings so feeling would eventually come back to the skin. I would hobble over to the arm bike on my crutches and crank my arms around on it as fast as I could, trying to raise my heart rate and break a mild sweat so I could feel somewhat like an athlete again. I found myself craving the exercise-induced endorphins that would flood through my body after an intense workout.

At the end of September, Dr. Mohtadi gave the okay for the right leg brace to come off, and a couple of weeks later I was on an airplane with Melissa headed to Toronto for a fundraiser. Everyone at the event had heard about my injury and was curious about how the recovery was coming along. "Very, very slowly," I answered. I ambitiously started the night on crutches, but had to transfer to a wheelchair mid-event because my legs were so fatigued.

In Toronto, we tacked on a couple of days to stay with Kelly and his family. It was so encouraging to be surrounded by his positive force once again.

Susan had lent me a travel-sized electrostimulation machine that fit into my backpack. The aim was to maximize every possible muscle-rebuilding moment. One evening, as I sat on the living room carpet with the web-like stimulation device contracting my quad muscles at random, Kelly leaned over and asked to take a closer look at the scars. The incisions were still a fresh shade of bright pink, and you could feel the threading of the stitches underneath the skin.

"How far can you bend your knees exactly?" Kelly asked.

The answer was not much. After a lot of work in the physio clinic, my right leg could now bend a whopping twenty degrees. I could lever the left a few degrees at most. To me, it didn't seem like much, but to Kelly, it was a cause for celebration.

"Look at that progress!" he exclaimed enthusiastically, a wide smile breaking over his face. "Now you just need to do that 20,000 more times! You'll be back to your old self in no time." I stared at him. He made it seem so simple. Kelly saw all the gloom of the situation, but in one sentence, he dissipated it. He took the one thing I could do and made it a positive. That set a tone for my recovery: in order to make this work, I needed to focus on all the things I could do, not all the things I couldn't.

All of those micro knee bends paid off. Four weeks later, at the end of October, Dr. Mohtadi gave me clearance to remove the left brace as well. With a satisfying rip and a little tugging, the black Velcro fell away and both of my legs were fully liberated for the first time in eight weeks. In the waiting room, Susan snapped a photo of me giving the final brace the bird. "See you never!" I told it.

At first, it felt like a monumental time in my life. I'd never questioned my ability to walk, yet suddenly I had a deep appreciation for it and everything else my body was capable of doing. My poor legs, though. They were so skinny and scrawny.

The muscle tone had dissolved, leaving me with the knobby knees of a ninety-five-year-old grandpa. Even without the braces, they stayed locked in a bent position as I stood, hard as lead pipes. Full range of motion would take some time to regain. But I was elated all the same, because I was finally free.

In those early days, every little thing I regained—walking, driving, doing a handstand—seemed massive. It was as if my life had been split into two time periods: B.I. (Before Injury) and A.I. (After Injury.) It was like reliving my childhood, because I got to do some of my firsts all over again, one of the best being my first night of sleep without a clunky brace getting tangled in the bed sheets. Everything around me seemed coated in a new layer of significance. Things I took for granted had been taken away, but now I started to have them back. This taste of progress supercharged my motivation and heightened my sense of self-awareness. I was so mindful of all the little things and appreciated them more than ever.

· · ·

The initial excitement began to fade around mid-December when the Tilt-A-Whirl of emotions took yet another turn. I'd be in the gym looking at the apparatus, still not able to do anything. It had been just over a month since the final brace came off, and even though I could now walk, I still couldn't do the simplest things in the sport, not even jump on a trampoline, because I hadn't yet built up the strength and mobility to do them safely. And that was particularly tough, because my favourite thing about gymnastics was always the doing-the-gymnastics part. It wasn't the physical prep and it certainly wasn't the conditioning.

It was sprinting down the vault runway and exploding over it, swinging and flying over the high bar, flipping from one corner of the floor to the other. And here I was, four months after the injury, and I still couldn't do any of those things yet. This wore my optimism thin, and with that mindset, it was only so long before I started despising the grind and feeling very sorry for myself.

The initial mobility gains may have stoked my inner fire, but as the progress began to taper off, rehab started to feel more like a chore. Physical therapy wasn't a day at the spa, no matter how patient and kind Susan tried to be. I could only take so many acupuncture needles to my inner thighs before I began to feel a little testy. My morning visits to the weight room, where trainer Mac Read had me do demanding exercises like wall sits with one leg for a minute at a time, left me shaking like a leaf. He knew that the only way to get my leg muscles back was to exhaust them. Ed, the team's massage therapist, grated his forearm across my hamstrings so deeply during our sessions that my fingers involuntarily gripped the edge of the table as I squirmed in pain. Dr. Gord McMorland, the team's chiropractor, realigned my entire body several times a week with a series of nauseating snaps, crackles, and pops. I'd come home after a day in this assembly line feeling like I wanted to crawl through the front door and straight into bed. In fact, some days I did just that.

When I wasn't on a physio table or in the weight room, I was in the gymnastics centre. There, Tony would stretch my shoulders and hips as I'd watch everyone else prepare for the upcoming season making real, tangible progress. I'd climb the rope and do handstand push-ups and chin-ups, but anything that really used my legs—in other words: almost everything—was still forbidden.

I secretly hoped that it would all come back easily, that I'd miraculously pick up again in the same shape as the day I got injured. But more than just my legs had weakened. The calluses had melted from my hands. My core strength was laughable. I felt like I'd never been a gymnast, never been to the Olympics. The visualizations I'd had of myself performing my routines in Beijing at the beginning of the comeback started to become blurry.

As day after day passed without any major improvements, I grew more and more discouraged. The Olympics were getting closer every day, but my progress seemed to be moving ahead in slow motion.

"I love a challenge. I love surprising myself and pushing myself to the limit. But now, that struggle seems like it is drowning me," I confessed on my blog.

As my positivity tank emptied, I became increasingly frustrated. I was so exasperated with my limitations, so over being injured, that one night over Christmas break I just put my forehead on the kitchen table and rolled it from side to side, practically writhing in defeat.

Mom gazed at me with mounting concern. "Can I ask you something?" she said, breaking into the moody silence. "Why are you putting yourself through this? You've already accomplished your ultimate goals. You've reached the pinnacle. You could stop it all right now and everyone would understand your decision. So *why* are you putting yourself through this?"

I stared at her. "Because this can't be the way my story ends," I said. "Two broken legs and then I'm done? No. That doesn't feel right. I can live with not making it back to the Olympics. But I can't live with not trying. Something inside of me won't let me accept that. What message does that send to everyone who's been following along? I can handle looking back in ten years and being disappointed if this doesn't work out, but I *cannot* handle the thought of looking back in ten years and regretting that I just gave up without trying. I have to try." It suddenly dawned on me how much I actually believed that.

I'd spent my career worrying: worrying about being the best, worrying about doing the numbers, worrying about what people thought of me, worrying about whether I was capable of achieving my goals. I always got validation in doing. No matter how much I doubted myself, I'd always been able to go into the gym, get to work, and confirm to myself that yes, I could do my tumbling passes. I could stick my landings. I could execute my routines. The injury had taken that away, and after nearly four months of not being able to do any gymnastics, I was unable to escape the negative thoughts that had taken root in my mind. But sitting at the kitchen table and being asked to connect with the purpose of all of this helped me feel refuelled.

. . .

As a child, I was pulled by the vision of getting to the Olympic Games. By 2007, though I was in good shape for the World Championships, something had been missing. The instant I broke my legs, all the superfluous stuff that had been floating around occupying space in my head disappeared and the blinders came down again. My eyes focused only on my end goal: getting back to the Olympics. Gymnastics was not something I *had* to do, it was something I *got* to do. And I certainly wasn't going to take the opportunity to do gymnastics for granted ever again.

It was the only explanation I had. The only why. I just had to keep trying.

After my conversation with Mom, I went to the local pool—not to swim, but to jump. I hadn't attempted any sort of jump into a landing since the day I broke my legs and I knew this was an important step in my journey back. I stood at the edge of the diving board and looked out at all the clear blue water below. It was a short way down, a metre at the most. I got myself all positioned to jump off, and then at the last second I froze. Some instinct was holding me back. I was afraid of the impact of going in feet first, even though it would be minimal.

My heart started pounding, and panic began crawling from my stomach up into my chest. *This isn't rational,* I told myself. *This isn't going to hurt at all. You can't do any damage. Your bones are healed.* All the same, I stood there like a statue, unable to bring myself to jump.

Is this a sign of things to come? I wondered. *If I can't jump feet first into a pool of water, how am I ever going to do a vault or tumbling pass and absorb the landing?*

The nightmares I'd been having since the injury had become more vivid as the Calgary winter came on. In those dreams, I was back in Stuttgart, getting ready to do the Tamayo. I would call Edouard over to watch and I'd stare toward the end of the floor. I would feel the sensation of taking off and doing the half turn in the air, but just before the landing, static would blare loudly through my mind and I'd bolt upright in bed, covered in sweat, heart racing a mile a minute.

With a little shake I returned to reality. The water lapped softly against the tile below. The first step was right in front of me. I counted to three, and with all the courage I could muster, leapt off into the pool. My feet broke the surface of the water, which closed around me as I fell. As I paddled back to the pool deck, it struck me that there was only one way to banish these negative thoughts. I needed to actually start doing some of those landings in the gym again.

24

THE GRIND

ANYONE WHO WATCHED ME STROLL DOWN A
hallway at the beginning of January 2008 would think I had
completely recovered. I walked normally, the spring literally
back in my step. But I was still unable to squat down or lay on my
stomach and lift my heels to my butt. I was still too afraid to land
on hard surfaces. Four months post-op, my big advancement
was having graduated to doing box jumps, jumping on and off
a mat that was only one foot above the ground. My less injured
right leg felt pretty strong, but the left didn't, and I didn't trust
it. Every landing felt like I was jumping onto one and a half legs.

Gym. Weight room. Physio clinic. As I rotated endlessly
between the three, I ran through the checklist in my mind.
Regain mobility and strength. Get my repertoire of skills back
and get back into gymnastics shape. Work up the endurance
to do full routines. Add the difficulty I'd need to challenge for
the Olympic floor title again. All in just eight months. And
what had been accomplished so far? Box jumps. Whoever would
have guessed that eight months before the Olympic Games I'd

be struggling with things four-year-olds are taught to do in kindergym?

"Some days I feel so overwhelmed," I confessed to Susan as she moved my left leg up and down like a water pump. "Every day the Olympics get closer. It's like there's a time bomb ticking down. And sometimes I'm stuck. Progress isn't happening as quickly as I'd like. I'm so far from where I should be."

"All you can do is do what you can do today," she replied, lowering my leg onto the table and picking up the other one. As she began moving it, she continued, "Today might not be as good as it was yesterday, but you never know what your next turn is going to be like. Ask yourself: what can I do today? Embrace it because today is what you've got. When you make the most of a lot of todays, you'll see that you're getting somewhere." She lowered my leg back onto the table. "Remember how you felt when you got your braces off?" I remembered, but that sense of freedom seemed like such a long time ago. "You've got to keep that perspective."

All you have is today. Add up the small progressions you make every day and you'll get somewhere. It was an elementary thought, but one with transformative power.

• • •

In mid-January, Melissa and I came to the conclusion that we were no longer on the same path, and after several painful discussions, we decided to go our separate ways. I returned to our home, but a For Sale sign was now staked into the front lawn. Tough as it was, I was able to put it into a box in my mind, close it, and not think about it. I avoided dealing with the emotional side of it, thinking that I had to put every ounce of energy I had into my comeback. I would unpack it later, I figured.

Around this same time, I did my first back handspring in five months, having gotten the thumbs up from Dr. Mohtadi to do some basic tumbling on soft mats. It hurt my knees a bit, but the pain wasn't excruciating. Moreover, it felt wonderful to bend backwards and turn my body over in the air, and being able to perform even the most basic of tumbling helped take my mind off my broken heart, at least during the hours I was in the gym. Within days, I had progressed from a single back handspring to four in a row. It was like riding a bike: my body knew exactly what to do.

At last, I felt a real sense of victory. "Who's on the comeback trail? That would be me," I crowed on my blog. "I can't even begin to explain how awesome it felt to be able to actually do some of the things that I would normally be able to do before the accident. It felt like a giant leap forward and an instant flood of confidence."

To my dismay, the giant leap forward lasted a single day. The next day I couldn't do anything, not even a single back handspring. The pain and stiffness in my legs was too much, and it took my body another two days to recover before I was able to do back handsprings again. A week later, I added front handsprings. Then saltos: flips where the hands don't touch the ground. The key was trusting my legs to punch me from the floor up into the air. Once up there, I was able to perform twisting skills without any problem.

Even with the first real leaps forward in the gym, there were still days when things just didn't work. There were many requests coming in for interviews, so my agency and I opened up

Wednesday mornings for media availability. This way we could funnel everyone into a specific window of time, and I could mentally prepare myself for the energy output it would require. I certainly didn't hold back when asked about the struggle. "I try to make them all good days, but it's impossible," I told one of my favourite journalists, Randy Starkman from the *Toronto Star*, when he came by the gym. "Some days are just really, really tough."

There were some positives to the process, I discovered. I got a boost out of filming my progress and posting it on my blog. Most often, Nathan was the one doing the filming, and his off-the-cuff commentary added an extra dimension to the videos. "Film this, film that," Nathan grumbled jokingly as I set up for my first really hard skill: a front layout with a double twist. I did make the skill, but the best part of the video is Nathan exclaiming "Look at those legs!" and zooming in on them as I walked back down the length of the floor trying not to look too pleased with myself. If I could do a front double full, that meant I could probably do a lot of other things.

At the beginning of February, I started working release skills again on high bar, putting in extra mats to land on in case things went awry. The Tkatchev, an element where the gymnast flies backwards over the bar before recatching it, was the first thing to come back. The first one I did, I caught the bar so smoothly you never would have been able to tell I hadn't done one in five months. I confidently walked over to the chalk bucket and plunged my hands into it, staring into space with a smile on my face. For the first time since that fateful morning in the training gym in Germany, I believed that making it to Beijing was actually possible.

The burning in my left leg persisted, though, threatening to stall my progress. Each time I landed, it felt like I had an interior bruise that someone had pushed on very hard, causing hot pain to radiate up my entire leg. Dr. Mohtadi decided to inject a local anaesthetic in the tendon at the very bottom of the plate in my knee to see if it would provide relief. It did, but only temporarily, and I was getting desperate for something a little more permanent. A few weeks later, another gigantic needle came toward my knee as I cringed with anticipation. This time it was a cortisone shot—the first and only of my career. God, that hurt! I winced and swore as the needle penetrated the skin. "The things I do for gymnastics," I groaned. Fortunately, it worked wonders: within a few days I could almost run like normal. With the edge of the pain taken off, my confidence in taking landings improved enormously. Getting the injection was very painful, but it turned out to be the right decision.

· · ·

When I was a kid, I was so serious about not missing practice that I convinced my parents to let me stay with my Grandma Trude in Calgary one Christmas while Scott went with them to visit Dad's family in Manitoba. With the competition season approaching, something as trivial as Christmas break wasn't an excuse to skip training, I thought.

As I sat on the beach in Maui and gazed out at the blue surf in the middle of February, the Olympic Games were less than six months away and I allowed my mind to wander back over the years, to question whether that one week of training had been *that* important. *Would I have made it to the Olympic Games if*

I had allowed myself to take my eyes off the final goal for even a second? Only here in Hawaii, twenty years after I'd started down the Olympic path, did I sit back, allow myself to enjoy the sunset, and admit that I wouldn't have lost all of my abilities in one week of vacation. That as committed as I was to the sport and the comeback I was attempting, it wasn't everything there was in life. At the end of the day, it was just gymnastics.

I was in Hawaii hosting a group of live auction winners from Gold Medal Plates (GMP), a series of charitable dinner events dedicated to raising funds for the Canadian Olympic Foundation. I had signed on to host the trip before the injury, thinking it would be a nice reward for a productive winter of training. Even in the throes of recovery, I felt the need to regroup and recover, to get away and cut loose just a bit. The Olympic grind would be waiting for me when I returned, and it would be more intense than ever.

So I took a week and went snorkelling and ziplining with the GMP crew, enjoying fancy meals prepared by Makoto Ono, the GMP championship-winning chef. I did make sure to do something physical every day, even if I had to get creative about it. I did bicep curls hoisting watermelons, and handstand presses on sand, as well as jogging and Pilates. Sometimes letting your mind relax can be integral to your recovery process.

When I arrived back in snowy Calgary, I found that I was able to physically do *more* after a week off than I had before I'd left. My range of motion had increased. I could do more squats and faster sprints. My mind felt rested and I returned with a new clarity about my place in gymnastics, too. As the Olympic champion, I had felt like there was a target on my back since Athens. I hadn't felt like the hunter anymore. But struggling to come back from this injury had forced me to change my perspective. I was finally chasing something again, and this was when I was at my best.

. . .

Like a rusty old truck revving up after sitting unused for a long period of time, I lumbered down the vault runway to do my first Yurchenko in seven months. My rhythm was off and the approach was sluggish, but by the time I pumped my arms up over my head and hurled into the roundoff, muscle memory had kicked in. Upside down, I punched off the table and into an easy laid-out backflip, flaring my arms open before landing on my feet and rolling backwards.

Being able to fly down a runway and flip over the vault was something I'd taken for granted before my injury, but at the March national team camp in Calgary, it felt phenomenal. Showing Edouard what I was able to do was even better, especially since I had barely been able to do a cartwheel at the January camp.

On my last day at camp, I sat down with him. Something was on my mind and I wanted him to know it. "Edouard, I don't want to be put on the Olympic team if I haven't earned my spot," I told him. "Please don't hand anything to me. I'm not here just to go to the Olympics to say I went. I'm here to be a contributing member of this team."

At the beginning of the year, when jumping twelve inches from a mat onto the floor seemed like an insurmountable challenge, I had seriously doubted my ability to come back and make the Olympic team. Being able to vault and tumble again opened my mind. As the snow melted and the Olympic spring bloomed over Canada, a blind belief that I was going to make it back to the Games gained traction in my mind, just like it had when I was nine years old. And for the first time since that morning in the Stuttgart training gym, I believed that I could also contend for a spot on the Olympic podium. That belief is what pulled me along.

25

THE PULL

RARELY DID A COMPLIMENT ESCAPE EDOUARD. When I landed my final dismount after performing all my routines in a private training session that June, however, Edouard gave a nod that spoke volumes.

By June, all of those "todays" where I made a little tiny bit of progress had added up to giant bounds forward. I had endured days where my legs felt like Jell-O and my knees screamed with the pain that came with the pounding, where I was so sore it hurt to breathe, where my mind spun in circles. Hearing the thud of my feet landing on the spring-loaded floor was a hurdle that had to be overcome. "The last time I heard a thud, my legs snapped. Thuds are not good," I wrote on my blog. I was putting so much effort in the gym that I was delirious outside of it. One Sunday I was so fatigued after training that when I went to my parents' for our weekly family dinner, I couldn't help but lay down face first on the linoleum floor in front of the fridge after the meal, unable to move. As I dozed off, my one-year-old cousin, Delaney, crawled on top of me, evidently curious if I was still alive. What felt like exhaustion, I knew, was progress in disguise.

Days after my twenty-sixth birthday in May, I landed my first double backflip since the injury. I was hesitant to stand up outright on the first several I did, opting to do safety rolls backwards rather than really absorb the landing through my legs. Once I did a few, I made the pleasant discovery that my legs could withstand the impact. That milestone accomplished, I realized all I needed to do was add a twist or two and have the stamina to do it at the end of the punishing seventy-second routine and I would be laughing. "It won't happen today or tomorrow," I wrote. "But it will when I need it to."

Once I had conquered my uncertainty about landing double saltos, I started putting together some sequences of multiple twisting elements in a row and building endurance by performing back-to-back floor routines comprised of basic elements. Those challenging three-minute efforts made me taste blood, but the satisfying burn in my lungs that comes at the end of a routine was something I hadn't known I missed.

I was particularly content the day I faced the Arabian double front for the first time. I did it in the easier piked position, cushioning my landing with a thick spongy mat. I vibrated with satisfaction after, knowing I had taken some of the power back from the skill that had haunted me ever since the injury.

. . .

The Canadian Gymnastics Championships are held in a different city each year, and at the beginning of that June they came to Calgary for the first time in fifteen years. It would have been a storybook comeback opportunity and there was some excitement about whether I would make my return to competition in my hometown, but I quietly withdrew a few days before the meet. Despite all the progress, I felt only about 75 percent ready. Though I fantasized about sticking dismounts and impressing my city, the thought of competing that week gave me a sinking feeling. My instincts were telling me that I wasn't quite ready yet, and I had learned to listen.

Instead, I put in a fabulous week of work inside the U of C gymnastics centre, and capped it off with an exclusive, by-invitation-only training session. The selective guest list included Edouard, Kelly, and Chris and Cindy Waller, who were all in town for the championships. I did my best to give them a show, treating it just like a competition. I presented a floor routine with full-difficulty middle passes bookended by simpler opening and closing runs, then did a handful of sky-high Arabian double front pikes and full-ins with extra landing mats to show that these skills were almost ready to be added back into my routine. I performed a full-difficulty rings set, and on vault treated my guests to five great Shewfelts, one after the other. When I landed my high bar dismount, Edouard gave me a satisfied nod.

"You look great," he said, and I glowed. I knew that I had done enough to merit an invitation to the first Olympic team selection camp, bypassing the championships. There was only one hurdle left to overcome. I may have been back on the Olympic track, but I still had to prove myself in a real competition.

· · ·

I had been pushing myself in the gym, trying to make up for lost time. Now that I could actually do some real gymnastics again, a familiar internal voice was urging me to go a little further. I needed to add difficulty to my floor routine if I wanted a legitimate shot at making it back up onto the Olympic podium. I would have to be better than I'd ever been, and while laying in bed one night in mid-June, I decided that I needed to add a brand-new element to my floor routine.

At the first Olympic trial, held at Capital City Gymnastics Centre in Edmonton, the blue floor carpet zoomed toward my head at an uncomfortable clip as I performed my new skill. I had completed one backflip in the straight-body position, initiated a half turn and was readying myself to roll out of the skill when I knew I wasn't where I needed to be.

For a fraction of a second, I panicked, but twenty years of training and a catlike air sense told me to commit. *Hold the flip*, my brain ordered. *You are not going out like this.*

One of the most popular elements on floor were rollout skills called Thomases, named for American Kurt Thomas, who originated them in the '70s. The idea was to go up into the air, execute flips and twists, and instead of coming down on your feet, go headfirst into the mat, tucking the chin to the chest and rolling smoothly out of the skill at the last second.

They looked cool, but Thomases were also one of the most dangerous things you could do in gymnastics. Because it's a floor mat and not a swimming pool, you literally risked a brain or neck injury every time you did one. I had tweety birds twirling around my head on a few occasions after mistimed attempts. But because it was such a risky skill, you got rewarded with difficulty points. So I, like a lot of people at that time, decided to perform it twice in my floor routine.

I mentally gritted my teeth and hung on, willing my skull not to slam into the mat. I was lucky: I actually overcooked the move, bouncing jerkily off of my back instead of smoothly rolling out of it. It may not have been elegant, but I was able to complete the routine unharmed.

"Man, you scared me with that one," Dave said afterward. He wasn't the only one. I shook my head like a horse. "I might have peed in my pants a little bit," I admitted. "But I've got to take it to the limit, man."

And I was. I was more focused than ever in the gym. Every practice pulled me toward my goal, but every practice also brought the Olympics half a day closer. I was doing the equivalent of an all-out sprint toward the finish line. My legs burned as I did the numbers necessary to stabilize a world-class routine on floor, and solid routines that would contribute to the team score on the other events. But I was satisfied, too: whatever the result, I was all in.

· · ·

The final Olympic trial was a homey affair held at the Calgary Gymnastics Centre in front of about 200 people. We performed our routines in a friendly atmosphere, cheered on by friends, family, and aspiring young gymnasts who hoped one day to be in our places.

The morning after the trials, we lined up side by side at the gym one last time. Edouard got right to the point. "I would like to announce that the 2008 Olympic team is Nathan, Adam, Grant,

David, Brandon ... and Kyle." And that was that. There were no fireworks or confetti cannons, just fist-bumps and high-fives. Hearing Edouard announce my name was especially satisfying. I had worked so hard for this one and felt I had earned my place.

· · ·

On July 26, I loaded my suitcase and gym bag into the back of my parents' SUV and they drove me to the airport. Destination: Beijing. As we cruised down Deerfoot Trail, all of the emotions lodged and suppressed over the past eleven months bubbled to the surface and suddenly I was a blubbering mess right there in the car. Dad kept looking back at me from the passenger seat and then over to Mom, raising his eyebrows and biting his lip. I was a twenty-six-year-old man bawling my face off. My parents didn't know what to say, but there really wasn't anything that needed to be said. I just needed to get it all out of my system before getting onto the plane.

Once in my seat, I would write in my journal and let it all go, but on the drive, I couldn't stop the tears from flowing. I was so proud of my journey back to Olympic form, but terrified of how I would measure up. The last time I had seen the international gymnastics community, I was in a wheelchair with my legs straight out in front of me. What would be my story of these Games?

26

BEIJING

ONCE MORE I STOOD IN THE CORNER OF THE floor, staring straight down the diagonal. The dimensions were the same as always, but for the first time in nearly a year, the soft landing mat that had been placed in the corner for every single landing wasn't there.

I took a deep breath and pushed down a small wave of fear. Doing a version of the skill that broke my legs still made me nervous. That's why I waited until we were in Beijing, on the day before podium training, to finally do one where it was just me and the floor, no security mat.

The first Arabian double pike onto the real floor was scary, but once it was out of the way I knew I was ready to compete. Completing my first tumbling pass with no mat was the last piece of my Olympic preparation puzzle, and it fell into place just in time.

· · ·

As always, men's gymnastics opened on the first day of the Games, so my Olympic opening ceremony attendance record became zero for three. I spent the evening on a physio table getting the final kinks kneaded out, then diving deeply into my journal in the room I was sharing with Nathan.

As a testament to how far I'd come, Edouard trusted me to lead the team off on rings, our first event in team qualification on August 9. It was the middle of the night back home, but I later heard that Canadians tuned in despite the extreme time difference. They had been bombarded with my story as the Olympic hype machine kicked into high gear, and as I landed that first dismount after a clean routine, I could almost feel a collective sigh of relief that my legs hadn't snapped in half again.

On vault, my Shewfelt was hands down the best of my career. High and with plenty of amplitude, I floated down to earth and landed softly, exactly where I needed to be. The stuck landing was so precise that even I was surprised. "Yesss!" I said, nodding my head. The words broke involuntarily from my lips before I turned to bow to the judges. I received an execution score of 9.75, the highest of the entire qualification competition. My second vault, the Kasamatsu full, was clean, but the difficulty value was lower than many top contenders, and the average was unlikely to propel me into finals. I just hadn't had enough time to build up to a more difficult second vault.

My heart jumped into my throat as I caught the Def on my fingertips on high bar, causing my legs to fly apart. It was not the textbook routine I wanted to deliver, but sometimes you have to take what comes. I landed my dismount, saluted the judges and took off my grips. In our black uniforms emblazoned with a white maple leaf and the five Olympic rings on the chest, we marched on to floor.

I was almost shivering with anticipation as we warmed up. This was the moment that pulled me along. I stayed focused by visualizing my routine and practising the corner parts on the sidelines. I also kept glancing at Susan and getting these waves of gratitude for everything she'd done for me from the moment I crashed on the floor in the training gym in Stuttgart. She'd been an adviser and advocate, but most of all she'd been a true friend.

One last time that day, I climbed the stairs to the competition podium and felt that strange, terrible, wonderful rush of emotions that comes as you stand ready to present yourself to the judges at the Olympic Games and show the world what you're really capable of.

"You're nervous because you care. This is important to you. Trust that those nerves are going to help you be great when you need to be. Don't run away from them. Use them as your superpower," Kelly always said.

The green light came on and I raised my arm.

. . .

Despite my efforts, the floor final was out of reach. The routine was very, very good, the best since the one I'd done that morning just before my injury. I was especially proud of it because it was the most difficult routine of my entire career in terms of the actual skill content. The additional Thomas tumbling pass I had added in the final push made for a total of six passes.

As a final flourish, I dismounted with the double twisting double back, the first and only time I'd done that difficult pass at the end of a full routine in eleven months. Going for it in the competition was a calculated move, because I wanted to max out my difficulty value. I felt I needed to include every tenth of extra difficulty I could manage in order to compete with the top guys. And though I landed it with my chest low and took a substantial step to the side, a consequence of not doing it at the end of my routine in any of the trainings beforehand, I was pleased with the effort. I truly did leave it all out on the floor.

Edouard and Tony were happy. So was Susan. After high-fiving my teammates and coaches, I walked up to Susan and gave her a long hug. "Thank you," I murmured into her ear. I pictured her taking the braces off my legs that first morning after the accident. "Thank you. Thank you."

We'd been in sixth place after our subdivision, but some of the best teams competed after us. We cherished the hope of remaining in the top eight, but deep down we knew it was unlikely.

Under the new scoring system, I received a 15.525 for my floor routine, which put me ninth as we left the arena. I hadn't seen the final scoreboard and learned my fate in the mixed zone right after the session, when a reporter framed her question this way: "A day of mixed emotions, Kyle. You came back from two broken legs to compete at the Olympic Games, but you won't be moving on to the floor final to defend your title. Tell me what you're feeling in this moment?" and my heart both beamed and broke simultaneously.

· · ·

When we got back to the Village, I took a walk. It was a cloudy day in Beijing and the air felt still. I wandered aimlessly for a while, trying not to think too hard about anything and beginning to process all that had happened during the past eleven months. After a while, I circled back toward our residence. As I got closer, I saw a familiar profile standing in front of the building.

"How did it go?" said Hap, waving me over. He was there to work with the Canadian swimming team and I was thankful fate brought us together again in that moment. I gave him a half smile. "It was okay," I said.

Hap must have sensed my disappointment because he fixed me with one of his sports psychologist looks. "Are you satisfied with what you did?" he asked.

"Sort of," I sighed. "I thought my routine went great, and I went for the big dismount, but I didn't make the final." It hurt a little to say it out loud.

"I guess it just wasn't meant to be," I continued. "But I feel like I didn't live up to everyone's expectations, including mine. Olympic champion breaks both of his legs and returns to make the podium. That was supposed to be the story."

Hap stood back and looked at me. "Could you have done anything more?" he asked.

I considered the question. All the hours of rehab. All those weights and exercises and needles. "No," I said honestly. "I couldn't have done anything more."

"Well then," said Hap, the same way he used to say "Ah!" when I was a kid. "There's a quote from great UCLA basketball coach John Wooden. I'm paraphrasing here, but it goes something like this: Success is a peace of mind, a sense of self-satisfaction in knowing that you did your best to become the best you are capable of becoming." He paused, leaned in, and looked me straight in the eye. "I know we are at the Olympics, and a lot of people are talking about winning medals and that being the only path to success, but that simply isn't true. If you can stand here today and say that you did everything you possibly could have done in your comeback to be at your best, *that* is success, Kyle. It's not just about making finals and winning medals. Success is defined from within. It's a feeling you get, and only *you* have the internal compass to measure what success feels like for you."

I'd like to say that made everything okay and I immediately became a shiny, happy daffodil afterwards. Real life doesn't work like that, though. While I contemplated the truth behind his words, I couldn't shake that my very best just hadn't been good enough, and I was ashamed. I thought of all the people who had supported me, and felt like I had let them down.

The headline in one of the Canadian newspapers the next day seemed to confirm my fears. "Shewfelt Fails in Comeback" was the A1 headline.

That morning, I had the opportunity to go on the CBC Olympic Primetime show with Ron Maclean to put a period at the end of my 2008 Olympic sentence. I half expected to be asked for an explanation as to why I hadn't made the final, but Ron didn't go there. Instead, he read a letter that the network had received from a mother named Krista in Calgary.

"All of our four kids and I stayed up for the duration last night to watch the men's qualification," she wrote. "It was a little surreal being that late at night, so quiet. It seemed like you were in our playroom, quietly doing your routines.

"Having met you, read your blog all year and seen you train and compete in Calgary, my heart was just bursting the whole time. You looked so focused and ready, but still so real that the kids could relate to you. Somehow that was as important or more important than the stellar quality of your routines.

"You gave way more to Canada and to individual gymnasts, kids, families and fans than you will be able to grasp for some time, I think. When kids see someone real, with real character and real team leadership and kindness, it stays with them far longer than seeing someone nail a routine and ultimately win a medal."

I felt my eyes welling up with tears, and it was all I could do not to break down right there in the studio. I pictured my ten-year-old self lounging on the carpet in my aunt and uncle's living room in Manitoba watching every second of the Barcelona Games. I thought about how enthralling the Olympics had always been for me, how inspired I'd been by all the athletes, how my idols and their accomplishments had propelled me forward.

If one family felt that way about what I had done, it had all been worth it. Success comes in many forms, one of which is a gold medal. But it's not the only one.

．．．

I was getting ready to leave the production studio when Scott Moore, the president of CBC Sports, poked his head out into the hallway. "Kyle, come in here a minute," he said, waving me into his office.

"Great interview just now," Scott said, settling himself behind his desk. "You've made us all really proud with your performance yesterday and the way you handled yourself in this comeback. You inspired a lot of Canadians." He paused for a moment and then said, "Say, have you ever thought about doing commentary?"

"Oh yeah!" I exclaimed. "Ever since I was a little kid." I thought back to my endless collection of gymnastics videos and the long list of commentator voices I admired chimed in my mind.

"Would you ever consider doing it for CBC?"

Commentating for CBC? Really? "Absolutely. It's always been a dream of mine," I exclaimed.

"How would you like to start tomorrow night with the men's team final alongside Lori and Brenda?" Scott said. Lori Strong-Ballard, a two-time Canadian Olympian, was the expert analyst, and Brenda Irving called the play-by-play.

"Sure," I blurted. *Is this for real?*

"That's great," Scott continued. "Just remember that there'll be millions of people watching, so you can't drop any F-bombs, but other than that, just be yourself. We'll get it all set up."

• • •

The training hall was quiet when I arrived the next day. We finished ninth as a team, barely missing the cut-off for finals, but Nathan and Adam did advance to the all-around final. I ended up ninth on vault and eleventh on floor, landing in the first and third reserve positions, respectively. I knew that I should be prepared just in case there were any last-minute withdrawals, but the thought made me cringe. People seldom pulled out of Olympic finals, even if tape was the only thing holding them together at that point.

I went onto the floor and did some light conditioning and stretching, but no real gymnastics. Everything hurt. My left wrist was so sore that I couldn't put it down to do a handstand.

My left leg burned more than ever when I tried to run. But something else was missing, something that had never been missing before: a reason to be there.

While Adam and Nathan trained, Tony and Susan and I spoke quietly about the future. For so long, Beijing had been the only thing in front of me, but suddenly it was behind me. Together, we weighed my options. Maybe I could take a couple of weeks off and return to do the fall world cup circuit? We had put in so much work to get back to a world-class level and it seemed wasteful not to continue. I thought back to the goal list I made in the eleventh grade. I had accomplished all of my major goals, except for one. I hadn't won a world title, but the thought of chasing it now left me feeling absolutely nothing.

Gazing around that Olympic gymnasium as Nathan and Adam trained, it slowly dawned on me that this was the last training session I'd ever attend. I just knew. It was the third day of the Games, but my competitive career in elite gymnastics was at an end. I was looking forward to making my commentary debut with CBC that evening, then to the days ahead, where we would be free to eat fistfuls of free Snickers bars and stay out late into the night.

27

TRANSITION

AT THE END OF AUGUST, I CAME HOME TO AN empty new condo and a barren life. Melissa and I had sold our home and almost everything in it that spring. I had a couch, a computer, a mattress on the floor, and that was pretty much it. For twenty years, my life revolved around gymnastics and getting to the Olympic Games. I had not really considered what I would do when they were over, and come the fall of 2008, I felt I had nothing to look forward to.

As the days grew shorter, depression hit me hard. When you return from the Olympics after not making the podium, there are no crowds of people who meet you at the airport. There are no helicopter rides or parades. Life resumes its course, except it doesn't. My new normal no longer included daily trips to the training centre, and without it I was completely lost.

I began spending lots of time alone, self-loathing and lethargic. One afternoon, I lay in a ball on my bed weeping for an hour before I had to leave to give a keynote speech on leadership for a group of business executives. *I can't do this*, I thought.

Of course, I did. I got up from under the covers and put on my suit and was full of pep as I delivered the speech. I was able to compartmentalize the depression to do the things that needed to be done. It was all the time in between that was destroying me. I waited all day for an email or a phone call with an invitation to my next gig. I had nothing else to do, no idea how else to live.

Being physical had always been my escape, but I didn't feel any spark to move my body. I would sit around all day and beat myself up for not being able to motivate myself to exercise. Months earlier, I had sprung out of bed at the crack of dawn ready to attack the day, but now I felt like I was walking through quicksand. Sometimes, after going back and forth in my head for hours, I would finally drag myself to the stairs of my condo building and run them, just to feel like I did *something*. Running those stairs, surrounded by the concrete walls and with no light at the end of the tunnel, seemed to symbolize the struggle perfectly.

When I wasn't lying in bed for days on end, I partied. Often it was with people I didn't know well because they couldn't compare me to my former self. "Let's go out and have a good time!" I said enthusiastically one evening to a group I'd briefly met at a fundraiser. The night ended at 4 a.m. and I had a huge hangover the next day. It was the first of several nights like that. I was trying to fill the void gymnastics had left and I had no idea how.

"So what do you do?" That was a hard question to answer, and I heard it a lot. "Well, I *was* a gymnast," I'd say. It was the only response I had. That would distract them enough that they didn't realize I hadn't really given a response.

Part of the problem was that I just couldn't admit to anyone how rotten I felt. *Nobody wants to hear it*, I thought. *They want upbeat, motivating things.* I was paying my bills as a motivational speaker and I knew that people wanted to hear positive things from a bubbly, happy personality. What they wanted to hear was how I was moving on and chasing my next dream. They didn't want to hear that I was struggling with depression—that would have put a buzzkill on any event. But this felt like an obstacle I couldn't overcome by myself.

At the end of October, I decided to take a writing course. One of our assignments was to write a detailed description of an image that depicted a white-capped mountain with blue sky in the background. We could go in any direction we desired. Some people focused on the accomplishment of reaching the peak. Some touched on the climbing experience and the senses it ignited. Mine turned into something morbid, but it was a true reflection of where I was mentally.

> I put everything I had into conquering this massive beast. It meant the world to me. The vision I had of myself alone at the peak of existence, brilliant blue sky and crisp, tingling air touching my face was incredible. The journey to the top was beautiful. The challenge was overwhelming, consuming, and it drove me beyond my preconceived limits. But now, as I am perched on an ash-coloured boulder, I feel alone. I don't feel the serenity, solitude, and calmness I expected. I feel empty and anxious. My toes are frozen. My heart is heavy. I am

disappointed in myself because I have reached
the ultimate and I can't appreciate its marvel.
Instead of being silent and content, breathing
in every ounce of this dream, I am fixated on
what comes next and how in the world I will
make my way down.

After sharing this on my blog, perhaps as a cry for help,
Marnie McBean, the Olympic champion rower and Team
Canada athlete mentor, reached out and asked if I was okay.
We connected and she reflected on her own transition out of
competitive sport and how it was a lonely and challenging time.
She provided some nuggets of advice, including this one that
really resonated: nothing will ever feel the same as chasing an
Olympic dream did, so stop looking for that *same* feeling. A new
feeling of purpose will eventually spark. Be patient.

Knowing that she struggled too made me feel less alone,
yet the sadness just wouldn't go away. A month later, after I
had another operation to remove the irritating plate and screws
from my left leg, I had some of my closest friends over for a
Friendsgiving feast. We drank margaritas from the plastic jar
I'd been given in Stuttgart, ate, and made tinfoil turkey hats to
wear on our heads. I didn't tell any of them of the darkness I was
experiencing. I didn't know how to. I put on the smile of Kyle
and pretended life was peachy.

At the beginning of December, I went back to Hawaii with
a friend for a two-week getaway. I thought being near an ocean
and palm trees again would brighten my spirits, but the feeling
of emptiness floated with me. I was riding a roller coaster of
emotions, and when I returned home, just before Christmas, I

spent four days in bed. I didn't even get up to eat or shower or watch TV. Occasionally, I would mope over to the bathroom mirror and stare at my body, wondering where my pecs were disappearing to. I kept the blinds closed and couldn't stop thinking that there was no one in the world who knew or cared what I was doing in that moment. But there was one person who had me in her thoughts. After a few days of not hearing from me, Mom called.

"When's the last time you got up?" she asked.

"Monday, I think," I replied. It was Thursday.

"Have you really just been lying in bed for four days?"

"Pretty much," I said.

"I'm coming over right now," she said. The phone clicked, and fifteen minutes later she was knocking on my door.

When she arrived, it all spilled out: the sadness that it was all over, that I had poured my heart into something for so many years and now had nothing left to do. I told her how I missed my coaches and teammates and didn't feel like I belonged anywhere. I shared my fear that I'd never find something else to fill that void. "I'm afraid I'll never be *good* at something again," I confessed.

Mom sat beside the bed and listened. Occasionally she put her arms around me like I was six again, trying to make it all okay. She nodded in agreement and let a few tears of her own fall. It's said that a parent can feel their child's pain, and she was mourning the loss with me. In the end, she gently suggested that I needed to reach out for help. Things weren't going to get better on their own.

Finally, I ended up in a place of security: Hap's green leather chair. Even making the appointment was hard, because I was so convinced that what I was feeling was somehow wrong, and that made me feel guilty. Hap understood completely. "You were flying on a trapeze that you've been holding on to for your whole life," he said. "And you've let go and you're falling through the air flipping wildly and you don't like it because you don't know when and where you're going to land. My advice to you is to choose a landing spot and get your feet on the ground again."

"What if it's not the right landing place?" The ever-present perfectionist in me stirred.

"It probably won't be, but nothing is permanent. You might not like it and maybe eventually you'll veer toward something else," he said. "But right now, you're in freefall, and until you've got two feet on the ground you're not going to be able to move forward. You can't gain momentum if you don't have anything to push off of."

The one thing I really looked forward to during this time was an evening yoga class at a local studio called Yoga Mandala. It gave me a brief respite from the new daily routine of laying on the couch and loathing myself. On a blizzardy Wednesday night at the beginning of January, I dragged myself out of bed and to the studio after a five-minute argument with myself about whether or not I should go. But I did go and something wonderful happened.

Because of the stormy weather, there were only five people in the class, including a woman I'd never seen before. She was just back from a vacation, with a golden tan and the funkiest pixie haircut. She was wearing a pair of pink, brown, and orange argyle socks that made her stand out, and she laughed with everybody. She had beautiful flowing movements into and out of her poses and I kept trying to sneak looks at her throughout the class, even though our mats were several metres apart. I watched to see the way she placed her feet on the mat, but my mind kept going back to that laugh. *I like her laugh*, I thought.

Since I was still very flexible from gymnastics, I thought I was great at yoga. Holding my leg over my head was not a challenge. A bridge was nothing. Handstands were my jam. I breezed through the class, congratulating myself the whole time. When it was over, the woman came over to me.

"I know who you are," she said. "I've figured it out."

"Sorry?" I said. *She's talking to me,* I thought.

"You're Kyle, that gymnast guy," she said. "This whole class I've been watching you lift your leg up to here"—she raised her arm over her head—"so you're definitely that gymnast guy."

"It's true," I admitted. *She knows who I am,* I thought.

"You're a freaking yoga cheater," she declared, pointing an accusatory finger in my face.

"What? What's a yoga cheater?"

"I was watching you and you have *no* idea what you're doing. You're just bendy."

"Well, maybe you should teach me how to do yoga then," I told her.

"Maybe I will," she said.

. . .

Her name was Kristin. I found that out when she added me on Facebook that night. A message came with the friend invite: "Hey, it was good to meet you. A group of us go out on Wednesday night after class. You should join us—we could all get to know you better . . ."

Yoga turned out to be my landing pad. Going to class gave my day some structure, and seeing Kristin there was always a bonus. I also started taking a life coaching course through the Coaches Training Institute, and I needed guinea pigs, giving me an excuse to talk to her more.

"Want to be my client? It'll be free. I'm taking a course and I need someone to practice my coaching on," I asked Kristin one night.

"Sure," she said. So I went over to her condo that weekend and we talked about the wheel of life and career planning and other things. "I have some wine and cheese if you want to hang out," she said afterward.

"Sure," I said, and she pulled out a spread of food that was definitely sprinkled with forethought.

The weekend after that, we spontaneously ended up at an after-hours club until 5 a.m. "You're coming home with me," she giggled as the night was winding down. I didn't need to be coaxed. "Okay!" I said agreeably. At 9 a.m., she kicked me out of her bed. "Go home," she told me, matter-of-factly. "My head hurts and I can't deal with you right now."

After that we were inseparable. We went ice skating and spent evenings and weekends going to brunch and roaming bookstores and hanging out at coffee shops. As we gazed at the travel section of a bookstore on Calgary's popular 17th Avenue one day in March, I had an epiphany. "I need to go on a trip," I told her. "Get out of here for a while. With a backpack and no plan."

"Yeah, me too," she said. "Where should we go?" We mulled it over for a few minutes and decided that Thailand was the place. We went back to her condo, booked flights to

Bangkok using airline points and left two weeks later. Kristin took a leave of absence from her job as an interior designer for the entire month of April and we wound our way around the country, eating pad see ew and massaman curry, attending full-moon parties, riding elephants, getting massages and pedicures, and doing yoga on the beach. We had no itinerary and our only requirement was that the room had to have air conditioning.

They say that if you want to test the strength of a relationship, you should travel together. We passed the test with flying colours. We were a great team and we learned to communicate and anticipate each other's needs. Because she didn't know me when I was training full-time, I was able to start defining myself more as Kyle the person rather than Kyle the gymnast.

I journaled a lot on this trip and came to the conclusion that I needed to make a formal retirement announcement upon our return. It was the only way I could start getting some closure and truly move on.

We were sitting drinking a Singha beer on the beach in Phuket on our last night when I asked her, "What happens now?"

"Well," she said, "you're my person, I know that. So take your time and I'll wait while you figure yourself out."

"All right," I said. We flew to Seoul together and then on separate flights back to Calgary. By 1 p.m. the day after we got back, I was on the phone with her, just because it seemed like it had been so long since we had talked and I had so much to tell her. After that I basically moved into her condo and attached myself to her at the hip. On January 9, 2016, almost seven years exactly to the day we met, our daughter Nora was born. Raising her has been our most exciting adventure.

. . .

At the end of May 2009, I officially retired from gymnastics. Still bronzed from the Thai sun and dressed in a grey suit, I made the announcement at a press conference at the Olympic Oval at the University of Calgary, the same venue where I met with the media a few days after my surgery. It was a bittersweet day, but it provided the closure that I needed to start looking forward. It was time to write my next chapter.

28

LEGACY

42.2 KILOMETRES. A FULL MARATHON. THINKING that my legs could carry me that distance seemed impossible, so of course I had to try.

I was built for power, not endurance. I was used to running 24.65 metres full speed toward the vault and then flipping over it. Doing this 1,700 times would equal the marathon distance. Long-distance running was not on my radar during my gymnastics career, but as I searched for some new direction in my life, chasing down an entirely new far-reaching athletic goal inspired me. Not only would it give me the physical release I was craving, it would give my days some shape. I desperately wanted to prove to myself that the characteristics that helped me achieve success in gymnastics could help me accomplish other goals in life. So I laced up my shoes and started running.

It began with the Stampede Road Race in Calgary, my first five-kilometre race. Partway through the course, someone ran past me and said, "Hey, I'm beating Kyle Shewfelt!"

"Congratulations, buddy! Remember, I was a gymnast, not a runner!" I hollered after him. I didn't need to win—committing myself to the training and pushing myself to finish as fast as I could was my goal. I finished somewhere in the middle of the pack for my age category, but crossing that first finish line came with a familiar sense of accomplishment that I hadn't felt in a while. And it felt good.

Next, I tried some 10-kilometre races on for size, then graduated to the half marathon (21.1 km). These distances hurt a little more toward the end, similar to those high bar routines done with bleeding hands, but I knew the pain was manageable. I liked the feeling of training for something again. It felt good to check off the "accomplished" box at the end of the day and to feel myself making measured progress. Some friends and I started a running group, and when the little devil would appear on my shoulder spewing excuses for skipping a run, I would have a more powerful force to latch on to: accountability. The inner voice that gains strength is the voice that you feed.

As 2011 gave way to 2012, I made the commitment to complete a full marathon. I narrowed my focus and started putting in more miles. I would go for long Sunday runs with my friend Martin Parnell, a fifty-seven-year-old ultra-marathoner and ambassador for Right To Play, a global organization that uses the transformative power of play to educate and empower children facing adversity. Martin had run 250 marathons in one year (yes, in only *one* year!) to raise over $1M for Right To Play, and he was a huge inspiration to me. We were both raising money for the organization through the Calgary Marathon's charity challenge and would meet at the Good Earth Coffeehouse at Eau Claire Market and run along the pathways beside the Bow River. I loved our conversations about the twists and turns of life. Martin joked that if you can't solve a problem during a five-hour-long run with a friend, then the problem doesn't have a solution. His always positive perspective and focus on giving back made me want to be better.

When I crossed the Calgary Marathon's finish line at the grandstand in Stampede Park, I learned two things about myself:

First: if I put my mind to something, I will do it!

Second: I don't need to run a marathon again! The last seven kilometres were downright excruciating and I didn't need to voluntarily suffer through that type of discomfort ever again. By the end, I had to clasp my hands under my thighs and hoist my legs up over the six-inch-high street curbs—my hip flexors and leg muscles felt very much like the cement I had spent the last three and a half hours running on.

Although uncomfortable, checking this item off my bucket list renewed my sense of belief in myself. It was confirmation that if I narrowed my focus in on a goal, made a plan, and surrounded myself with accountability and support, I could accomplish anything, even outside of the gym.

· · ·

During the three years after my official retirement announcement, I followed Hap's advice and kept trying professional things on for size, hoping to gain traction. I completed my life coach training. I started working toward getting a real estate licence. I went back to school at Mount Royal University and studied broadcast journalism and business with a focus on entrepreneurship. I continued motivational speaking and doing gymnastics commentary. If only there were more televised gymnastics events in Canada, I would have been in heaven.

I auditioned to host morning television shows. I emceed events and did a yoga teacher training course. Jean-Paul offered a paid ambassador role for Gymnastics Canada, where I would do promotions and make appearances at their events. Tony invited me to start the Kyle Shewfelt Gymnastics Festival in partnership with the University of Calgary Gymnastics Club. I was inducted into Canada's Sports Hall of Fame. I did corporate hosting at the 2010 Vancouver Olympic Games and I joined the board of directors for the Canadian Centre for Ethics in Sport as the athlete representative. I travelled to Monrovia, Liberia with Right To Play and deepened my commitment to the Special Olympics movement.

I did what felt like a thousand things, all of them good, yet I still didn't know where I was going. I simply hadn't found the professional landing spot that made me want to settle in and really get comfortable.

In the summer of 2012, CTV sent me to London to be their expert commentator for gymnastics. I had a wonderful time taking in the Games from the broadcast booth and returned home convinced of one thing: I needed gymnastics in my daily life again.

All along I'd thought that one day my involvement in the sport would come to an end and I'd move on and do something else. But then I'd come back to a question that was asked during my life coach training: when you think back on your childhood, what was the moment when you felt most excited? And for me, the moment that flashed through my mind was tumbling across the floor in the gym and flipping into the foam pit. It was the spark of pride and accomplishment when I mastered a new skill.

It was gymnastics. Always gymnastics.

· · ·

"Tell me about your work experience," the recruiter said, his pen poised over a yellow legal pad.

I cleared my throat nervously. "Well," I started, "I was a gymnast . . ."

It was the end of September 2012 and I was determined to get a day job. As much as I enjoyed speaking, commentating and all the other one-off gigs, I was going stir crazy between them. I needed consistency and thought a steady paycheck and health benefits would be nice too. I pictured myself doing something corporate, like community engagement, marketing, or communications. I hoped a recruiter could help make the necessary connections.

"Do you have any experience in a corporate setting?" the recruiter asked.

"I've done some motivational speaking in plenty of boardrooms," I replied, sensing that that wasn't the right answer.

When I got back out onto the street, I loosened my tie, looked up into the blue sky, and let out an anxious sigh. I decided to walk the thirty blocks home so I could decompress and think. Sunlight shone through the gaps between the downtown office buildings at each crosswalk I approached. The session with the recruiter had been rougher than I thought it would be. I couldn't shake the feeling that it was all wrong, like I was trying to be someone else, stretching my experience and interests and moulding them to fit job descriptions that weren't right for me.

As I walked along, it dawned on me that I didn't actually want to work for someone else. Yes, I wanted stability, but I am an entrepreneurial spirit and I like being in charge of my own destiny. Gymnastics is what makes me happiest. I wanted to make a positive impact in the community and build a legacy. When I looked at things that way, the question of what to do next practically answered itself.

"I'm going to open a gym," I announced to Kristin about two seconds after walking in the door. I took out my phone and looked up Krystal, a former Altadore coach whom I'd been friends with during my time there. We'd kept in touch and I knew she had left the gymnastics world to focus on raising her two young sons.

"Yo Krystal, it's Kyle," I said when she answered. "I'm going to open a gym. I know that we've talked about this when we were younger, but it's finally happening. Do you want to be my program director?" There was a pause at the end of the line, and then she said, in her boisterous and bubbly way, "Hells yeah I do!"

· · ·

It's one thing to have an idea, but another to bring it to life.

I knew right away that I didn't want to train Olympic athletes. That might sound strange given that competing and the Olympics made up a huge part of my gymnastics experience, but I chose to focus on the grassroots side. I wanted to create the spark for as many students as possible to be exposed to the sport and for it to be seen as a key foundation for an active and healthy future.

There were already several gyms in the Calgary area and throughout Canada dedicated to getting gymnasts to the highest competitive level. I decided to feed to them rather than compete with them. My gym wouldn't be about results and placements, but about creating a launching pad for success. I wanted to provide a space where kids and adults could do gymnastics alongside one another. That's what felt right, and so this vision became my guide.

Once the concept was in place, I really got to work. I had to build a business plan with strong financial projections, pitch to investors, and secure start-up capital. There was the task of getting a bank loan for equipment and building improvements and refining what exactly would be needed for the business to function. Kristin and Krystal served as sounding boards and helped put the pieces together.

We must have looked at twenty spaces before finding an industrial bay on the south side of Calgary near lots of residential neighbourhoods that was full of potential. Kristin and her sister Amber, also an interior designer, walked in, looked at the bare concrete floor and unpainted walls, and had a vision. "We can do something with this," they said confidently.

Together, we designed the way equipment would be laid out in the gym, as well as the front reception, offices, and viewing areas. As contractors did construction and began digging out the foam pits, Krystal and I designed a class schedule and recruited staff. We spent hours each day on the phone refining the details. Sometimes she'd lock herself in her closet in order to escape the chaos that came with raising two boys aged seven and five.

I was gladly "working" sixteen hours a day, because it didn't feel like work at all. My mind was like a firework display and I kept waking up in the middle of the night with new ideas and solutions. I began keeping a notebook next to my bed so I could capture them before they melted away. A friend also gifted me a set of waterproof paper called "Aqua Notes" that allowed me to jot down ideas even when I was in the shower!

Over the May long weekend, as my friends played bocce in the park, I sat at home putting the finishing touches on the business plan. Starting a gym had become a full-time obsession, much like doing gymnastics had been so many moons ago.

With ten days to go before the grand opening, my clothes were hanging off of me. I had been so busy staring at Excel spreadsheets, emailing vendors, confirming deadlines, and supervising the construction of the gym that I kept forgetting to eat. With so much to do, at times the finish line seemed impossibly far away. But when I looked at the successful gyms that some of my gymnastics idols—now good friends—had opened, I reminded myself that if they could do it, so could I. They had inspired me in gymnastics. Now they were inspiring me in business.

When the foam pits were dug and the building improvements complete, truckloads of Speith America gymnastics equipment backed up to the big bay doors at the back of the building. The outpouring of support to set up the gym overwhelmed me. Family, friends, and even friends of friends showed up to help. There was a small army of volunteers unloading trucks and building equipment. When the final roll of fuzzy blue floor exercise carpet was rolled out and Velcroed down, I did my first roundoff to a back tuck in over five years. It felt so satisfying to tumble again and to see the vision come to life.

• • •

The doors of Kyle Shewfelt Gymnastics opened on Monday, October 28, 2013. That day, kids and their parents passed through an entryway emblazoned with words like "Joy," "Community," "Dream," and "High Five." We called it our inspiration wall and hoped it would set the tone for their experience with us. My dog Cooper, a Brittany spaniel whom we transformed into our cartoon dog mascot Super Cooper, was there wearing a red superdog cape, cleaning up Arrowroot cookie crumbs and sniffing everyone's faces. Our team frantically answered phones that rang off the hook and greeted people as they walked in the door. Krystal and I taught kindergym classes in the daytime, and in between I made runs to the local hardware store to pick up forgotten miscellaneous items.

My mind felt like it had a hundred browser tabs open and I was learning how to be a business owner on the fly. When classes began that evening, I led a group warm-up that was both challenging and fun, just the way Kelly always had when I was a little boy.

Toward the end of the day, I sat down at my desk and looked over the top of the computer through the plate-glass window that allowed me to see what was happening out in the gym. Children were running around on the floor, jumping in hula hoops, rolling down cheese-shaped wedge mats, swinging on bars, doing handstands against walls and bouncing on trampolines with glee radiating from their faces. Sounds of joy echoed throughout the space.

I closed my eyes, allowing my memory to drift back to my first experiences in the gym. My heart surged as I reconnected with the happiness I felt when I knew I had found my place. Once again I was flying, but I was no longer in freefall. I had spotted my landing and now, with two feet firmly on the ground, I was able to move forward by giving back. I could help create the same exhilaration and excitement for a new generation.

Yes, I thought, *this is exactly how this is meant to be.*

ACKNOWLEDGEMENTS

There have been many difference makers in my life, my gymnastics career, and in the creation of this book. I am extremely grateful to everyone who has put forth time and energy to help guide me along the way.

My daily foundation is built on the strength and support I receive from Kristin and Nora—my two favourite people. Thank you for your patience and understanding during this process. I had no idea how intense and consuming writing a book could be, but your love and kindness made it possible for me to see it through.

To Mom and Dad: thank you for providing me with the opportunity to pursue my passion and for never questioning my big dream. You've set the parenting gold-medal standard—I hope I can give Nora the same experience of unconditional love and support that you have given me.

To all of my friends and family, you know who you are and I love you all. A special thank you to my big brother Scott for teaching me how to do my first cartwheel.

To Kelly: I couldn't have reached my ultimate goals without you by my side. Thank you for your unwavering belief in me. Thank you for protecting me, for fueling me with positivity, and for bringing calm into those pressure cooker moments. Thank you to the universe for bringing us together.

In the more than twenty years that I was a gymnast, I met hundreds of special coaches—certainly too many to name here—but please know that I remember each of you and your contributions. A very special thank you to Tony, Uldi, Eugene and Edouard.

Thank you to my many teammates from Altadore, U of C and the provincial and national teams—you made gymnastics a place of fun, friendship and great memories.

Thank you to the Alberta Gymnastics Federation, Gymnastics Canada, the Canadian Olympic Committee, the Canadian Sport Institute, Bell Canada and every organization and person that contributed financial and behind-the-scenes support during my gymnastics career.

Thank you to our team at Kyle Shewfelt Gymnastics—I am so proud of what we are building!

Thank you to every journalist and media outlet that has taken interest in my journey. I appreciate that you've made time for me. A special thanks to the CBC, Scott Russell, Lori Strong-Ballard, Brenda Irving, and Randy Starkman (RIP).

OTHER BUSINESS

Reviews and referrals:
If reading this book has brought you joy or taught you something new, please consider leaving a positive five-star online review or telling a friend. Your referral makes a big difference!

Speaking and book signings:
To invite Kyle to speak or to host a book signing event, please send a request with details to info@kyleshewfelt.com.

SPECIAL OLYMPICS

**Special
Olympics
Olympiques
spéciaux**
Canada

A portion of the net proceeds from the sale of this book will be donated to Special Olympics Canada. These funds will help support the more than 47,000 Special Olympics athletes across the nation as they pursue their goals in both sport and life.

To learn more about Special Olympics programs, volunteer opportunities, and ways to give, please visit www.specialolympics.ca

CAREER HIGHLIGHTS

Olympics:
Three-time Olympian (2000, 2004, 2008)
2004 gold medal, men's exercise

World Championships:
2003 bronze medal, floor exercise
2003 bronze medal, vault
2006 bronze medal, floor exercise

Commonwealth Games:
2002 gold medal, floor exercise
2002 gold medal, vault
2002 silver medal, team
2006 gold medal, vault
2006 gold medal, team
2006 bronze medal, floor exercise

World Cup Finals:
2000 silver medal, floor
2002 silver medal, floor
2006 silver medal, floor

Awards and honours:
Lionel Conacher Award, 2004
Canadian Sport Awards, Male Athlete of the Year, 2005
Alberta Sports Hall of Fame, 2005
Canadian Sport Awards, Spirit of Sport Story of the Year, 2008
Canada's Sports Hall of Fame, 2010
Canadian Olympic Hall of Fame, 2014

ABOUT THE AUTHOR

A lifelong devotee of gymnastics since learning how to do a cartwheel as a young boy, three-time Olympian Kyle Shewfelt made history by winning gold on the floor exercise at the 2004 Athens Games, the first and only medal for a Canadian in artistic gymnastics. Today a motivational speaker, gym owner, broadcaster and father, Kyle believes his success stemmed from the positivity fostered by his parents, coaches and mentors that guided him throughout his career. Kyle is a member of Canada's Sports Hall of Fame and the Canadian Olympic Hall of Fame, and is a proud champion for Special Olympics. He resides in Calgary with his partner, Kristin, their daughter, Nora, and their dog, Cooper, and he continues to enjoy cartwheeling around the house.

Facebook: kyle.shewfelt
Twitter: @kyleshew
Instagram: @kyleshew

www.kyleshewfelt.com